NOT SAFE

MARK
BATTERSON

NEW YORK TIMES BESTSELLING AUTHOR

ZONDERVAN

Not Safe

Copyright © 2013 by Mark Batterson

Derived from material previously published in *All In*.

Abridged by Meredith Hinds

Requests for information should be addressed to:

Zondervan, 3900 Sparks Dr. SE, Grand Rapids, Michigan 49546

ISBN 978-0-310-63202-3 (hardcover)

ISBN 978-0-310-63203-0 (ebook)

Published in association with the literary agency of Fedd & Company, Inc., 606 Flamingo Boulevard, Austin, TX 78734.

Art direction: Jamie DeBruyn

Interior design: Mallory Collins

Printed in the United States of America

19 20 21 22 23 24 25 26 27 28 / LSC / 10 9 8 7 6 5 4 3 2 1

Dedicated to the church I have the joy and privilege of pastoring—National Community Church, Washington, DC

CONTENTS

NOT SAFE

NOT EASY

NOT HALFWAY

CONTENTS

NOT MY OWN

NOT AFRAID

PART ONE

NOT SAFE

ONE

PACK YOUR COFFIN

A century ago, a band of brave souls became known as one-way missionaries. Instead of suitcases, they packed their few earthly belongings into coffins. As they sailed out of port, they waved good-bye to everyone they loved, everything they knew. They knew they'd never return home.

A. W. Milne was one of those missionaries. He set sail for the New Hebrides in the South Pacific, knowing full well that the headhunters who lived there had martyred every missionary before him. His coffin was packed. For thirty-five years, he lived among that tribe and loved them. When he died, tribe members buried him in the middle of their village and inscribed this epitaph on his tombstone:

> When he came there was no light.
> When he left there was no darkness.

When did we start believing that God wants to send us to safe places to do easy things?

Jesus didn't die to keep us safe. He died to make us dangerous.

Faithfulness is not holding the fort. It's storming the gates of hell.

The will of God is not an insurance plan. It's a daring plan.

The complete surrender of your life to the cause of Christ isn't radical. It's normal.

Quit living as if the purpose of life is to arrive safely at death.

Pack your coffin.

TWO

THE INVERTED GOSPEL

In the sixteenth century, the Renaissance astronomer Nicholas Copernicus challenged the belief that the earth was the center of the universe. Copernicus argued that the sun didn't revolve around the earth, but rather that the earth revolved around the sun. The Copernican Revolution turned the scientific world upside down.

Each one of us needs to experience our own Copernican Revolution. The paradigm shift happens when we come to terms with the fact that the world doesn't revolve around us.

When we are born into this world, we're spoon-fed on the front end and diaper-changed on the back end. It's as if the entire world exists to meet our every need. And that's fine if you are a two-month-old baby. If you're twenty-two, it's a problem!

Newsflash: *You are not the center of the universe!*

At its core, sinfulness is selfishness. It's enthroning yourself—your desires, your needs, your plans—above all else. You may still seek God, but you don't seek Him first. You seek Him second or third or seventh. You may sing "Jesus at the center of it all," but what you really want is for people to bow down to you as you bow down to Christ. It's

5

a subtle form of selfishness that masquerades as spirituality, but it's not Christ-centric. It's me-centric. I call it the inverted gospel.

WHO'S FOLLOWING WHOM

Most people in most churches think they are following Jesus, but I'm not so sure. The reality is this: *they have invited Jesus to follow them*. They call Him Savior, but they've never surrendered to Him as Lord. And I was one of them. Trust me, I didn't want to go anywhere without Jesus right there behind me. But I wanted Jesus to follow me, to serve my purposes, to do my will.

It wasn't until I was a nineteen-year-old freshman at the University of Chicago that I had my Copernican Revolution. It started with this question: *Lord, what do You want me to do with my life?*

I got tired of calling the shots. I wasn't very good at playing God. I stopped trying to "find myself" and decided to seek God. I couldn't read His Word enough. I got up early to pray. I even fasted for the first time in my life. I meant business. For the first time in my life, I put Him first.

On the last day of summer vacation, I got up at the crack of dawn to do a prayer walk. Our family was vacationing at Lake Ida in Alexandria, Minnesota. The dirt road I walked down may as well have been the road to Emmaus. After months of asking, I finally got an answer to my question. I knew what God wanted me to do with my life.

On the first day of my sophomore year, I walked into the admissions office at the University of Chicago and told them

I was transferring to a Bible college to pursue full-time ministry. Giving up a full-ride scholarship to one of the top-ranked universities in the country didn't make much sense on paper. But I knew this was my no fear, now-or-never moment.

Was it a gut-wrenching decision? Yes. Did I ever second-guess it? More than once!

Let me ask the question: *Who's following whom?*

Are you following Jesus?

Or have you inverted the gospel by inviting Jesus to follow you?

HOLY DARE

More than a hundred years ago, a British revivalist issued a holy dare that would change a life, a city, and a generation. That timeless challenge echoes across every generation: "The world has yet to see what God will do with and for and through and in and by the man who is fully and wholly consecrated to Him."

The original hearer of that call to consecration was D. L. Moody. When those words hit his eardrums, they shot straight to his soul. That call to consecration defined his life. And his life, in turn, defined consecration.

It was Moody's all-in moment.

Maybe this is yours?

You are only one decision away from a totally different life. It will probably be the toughest decision you'll ever make. But if you have the courage to completely surrender yourself to the lordship of Jesus Christ, there is no telling what God will do.

D. L. Moody left an indelible imprint on his generation. In the late 1800s, his sermons contributed to a great spiritual awakening worldwide. And more than a century later, his passion for the gospel continues to indirectly influence millions of people through Moody Church, Moody Bible Institute, and Moody Publishers.

The world has yet to see what God will do with and for and through and in and by the man who is fully and wholly consecrated to Him.

Why not you?

Why not now?

AMAZING THINGS

Anytime God is about to do something amazing in our lives, He calls us to consecrate ourselves to Him. That pattern was established right before the Israelites crossed the Jordan River and conquered the Promised Land.

"Consecrate yourselves, for tomorrow the Lord will do amazing things among you."

Here's our fundamental problem: *we try to do God's job for Him.* We want to do amazing things for God. And that seems noble, but we've got it backward. God wants to do amazing things for us. That's His job. Our job is consecration. That's it.

Before I tell you what consecration is, let me tell you what it isn't.

It's not going to church once a week.

It's not daily devotions.

It's not keeping the Ten Commandments.

It's not sharing your faith with friends.

It's not giving God the tithe.

It's not volunteering for a ministry.

It's not going on a mission trip.

All of those are good things, but that isn't consecration.

The word *consecrate* means to *set yourself apart*. Consecration demands *full devotion*. It's dethroning yourself and enthroning Jesus Christ. It's giving God veto power. It's surrendering *your fear* out of *fear for Him*. Consecration is an ever-deepening love for Jesus, a childlike trust in the heavenly Father, and a blind obedience to the Holy Spirit.

NOT SAFE

My greatest concern as a pastor is that people can go to church every week of their lives and never go *all in* with Jesus Christ. I'm afraid we've cheapened the gospel by allowing people to stay safely on the sidelines. We've given people just enough Jesus to be bored but not enough to feel the surge of holy adrenaline that courses through your veins when you decide to follow Him.

You cannot be in the presence of God and be bored at the same time. For that matter, you cannot be in the will of God and be bored at the same time.

The choice is yours—consecration or boredom? If you don't consecrate yourself to Christ, you'll get bored. If you do, you won't. If you don't go all in, you'll never enter the Promised Land. But if you go all out, God will part the Jordan River so you can cross through on dry ground.

Stop trying to do God's job for Him. You don't have to do amazing things. You can't do amazing things. *Amazing always begins with consecration*. And just as amazing always begins with consecration, *consecration always ends with amazing*.

When you look back on your life, the greatest moments will be the moments when you weren't safe. It's as true today as it was the day Abraham placed Isaac on the altar, the day Jonathan climbed a cliff to fight the Philistines, and the day Peter got out of the boat and walked on water.

The longer I follow Jesus, the more convinced I am of this simple truth: God doesn't do what God does *because of* us. God does what God does *in spite of* us. All you have to do is stay out of the way.

It's that simple. It's that difficult.

Stay humble. Stay hungry.

If you aren't hungry for God, you are full of yourself. That's why God cannot fill you with His Spirit. But if you will empty yourself, if you will die to self, you'll be a different person by the time you reach the last page of this book. As I wrote this book, I prayed that God would rewrite your life. If you let go and let God take control, He'll write history, His Story, through your life.

THREE

DRAW THE LINE

"Take up your cross daily, and follow me."
LUKE 9:23 NLT

In AD 44, King Herod ordered that James the Greater be thrust through with a sword. He was the first of the apostles to be martyred. And so the bloodbath began. Luke was hung by the neck from an olive tree in Greece. Doubting Thomas was pierced with a pine spear, tortured with red-hot plates, and burned alive in India. In AD 54, the proconsul of Hierapolis had Philip tortured and crucified because his wife converted to Christianity while listening to Philip preach. Philip continued to preach while on the cross. Matthew was stabbed in the back in Ethiopia. Bartholomew was flogged to death in Armenia. James the Just was thrown off the southeast pinnacle of the temple in Jerusalem. After surviving the one-hundred-foot fall, he was clubbed to death by a mob. Simon the Zealot was crucified by a governor of Syria in AD 74. Judas Thaddeus was beaten to death with sticks in Mesopotamia. Matthias, who replaced Judas Iscariot, was stoned to death and then beheaded. And Peter was crucified upside down at his own request. John the Beloved is the only disciple to die of natural causes, but that's only because he survived his own execution. When a cauldron of boiling oil could not kill John, Emperor Diocletian exiled him to the island of Patmos. He then returned to Ephesus, where he wrote three epistles and died of natural causes about AD 100.

Every Christian living in a first-world country in the twenty-first century should read *Foxe's Book of Martyrs*. It redefines risk and sets the standard for sacrifice.

Our normal is so subnormal that normal seems radical.

In Luke 9:23–24, Jesus threw down the gauntlet with his disciples. He wanted to see who was in and who was out.

> *"Whoever wants to be my disciple must deny themselves and take up their cross daily and follow me. For whoever wants to save their life will lose it, but whoever loses their life for me will save it."*

The disciples took this literally. We can at least take it figuratively. If Jesus hung on His cross, we can certainly carry ours! And that isn't just our greatest responsibility. It's our highest privilege.

Anything less than the complete surrender of our lives to the lordship of Jesus Christ is robbing God of the glory He demands and deserves. It's also cheating ourselves out of the eternal reward God has reserved for us.

We won't come alive until we die to self. And we won't find ourselves until we lose ourselves in the cause of Christ.

If Jesus is not Lord *of all*, then Jesus is not Lord *at all*.

It's now or never.

It's not safe.

THE AMERICANIZED GOSPEL

We have Americanized the gospel or spiritualized the American Dream. Neither one comes close to the true gospel. When you try to add something to the gospel, you aren't enhancing it. The gospel is as good as it gets.

You only get a relationship with God on His terms. You can take it or leave it, but you cannot change the rules of engagement.

The apostle Paul defines the deal that is on the table this way:

God made him who had no sin to be sin for us, so that in him we might become the righteousness of God.

The moment you bow your knee to the lordship of Jesus Christ, all of your sin is transferred to Christ's account and paid in full. It was nailed to the cross two thousand years ago! But that's only half the gospel. Mercy is not getting what you deserve—the wrath of God. Grace is getting what you don't deserve—the righteousness of Christ. Everything you've done wrong is forgiven and forgotten. And everything Christ did right—His righteousness—is transferred to your account. And then God calls it even.

It's like God says, "I'll take the blame for everything you did wrong and give you credit for everything I did right." It's not just good news. It's the best news.

The gospel costs nothing. It can only be received as a free gift, compliments of God's grace. So it costs nothing, but it demands everything. And that is where most of us get stuck. We're too Christian to enjoy sin and too sinful to enjoy Christ.

We want everything God has to offer without giving

anything up. We want to buy in without selling out. We're afraid that if we don't hold out on God, we'll miss out on what this life has to offer. It's a lie. It's the same lie the serpent told Adam and Eve in the garden. God is not holding out on you.

You can take Psalm 84:11 to the bank:

> No good thing does God withhold from those who walk uprightly.

If you don't hold out on God, I can promise you this: God will not hold out on you.

NO SACRIFICE

I don't think anyone has ever sacrificed anything for God. If you get back more than you gave up, have you sacrificed anything at all? The eternal reward always outweighs the temporal sacrifice. At the end of the day, Judgment Day, our only regret will be whatever we didn't give back to God.

The key to self-fulfillment is self-denial. Self-denial is shorthand for delayed gratification. And by delay, I don't mean days or months or years. I mean a lifetime. Our delayed gratification on earth translates into eternal glory in heaven.

The selfish part of us has an allergic reaction to the word *deny*. We don't just tolerate indulgence in our culture. We celebrate it. But the fundamental problem with indulgence is that *enough is never enough*. It's not until we go *all in* with God that we discover that true joy is only found on the sacrificial side of life.

The more you give away, the more you will enjoy what you have. If you give God the tithe, you'll enjoy the 90 percent you keep 10 percent more. You'll also discover that God can do more with 90 percent than you can do with 100 percent. If you double tithe, you'll enjoy the 80 percent you keep 20 percent more! One of our life goals as a family is to reverse tithe and live off 10 percent while giving away 90 percent. When we get there, I'm confident we'll enjoy the 10 percent we keep 90 percent more.

Most of us spend most of our lives accumulating the wrong things. We've bought into the consumerist lie that *more is more*. We mistakenly think that the more we give, the less we'll have. But in God's upside-down economy, you ultimately lose whatever you keep and you ultimately keep whatever you lose for the cause of Christ.

THE RICH YOUNG RULER

On paper, the Rich Young Ruler was the epitome of religiosity. But religiosity and hypocrisy are kissing cousins. The Rich Young Ruler is the antitype of all in. And his life is a standing warning: *if we hold out on God, we'll miss out on everything God wants to do in us, for us, and through us.*

I haven't met many people possessed by a demon, but I've met a lot of people possessed by their possessions. And that is certainly true of the Rich Young Ruler. He had everything money could buy. He had his whole life in front of him. And he called his own shots. Yet something was missing. He asked Jesus:

What am I still missing?

The Rich Young Ruler had everything we think we want. He was rich. He was young. And he was in a position of power.

Why was he so miserable? The answer is easy: he was *following the rules*, but he wasn't *following Jesus*.

The text tells us he kept *all* the commandments. But righteousness is doing something right. We've reduced it to doing nothing wrong.

We fixate on sins of commission: *Don't do this, don't do that—and you're OK*. But that is holiness by subtraction. It's the sins of omission—what you would have, could have, and should have done—that break the heart of your heavenly Father.

The heavenly Father is preparing good works in advance with our name on them. But we can't just play defense. We have to play offense! We can't just do nothing wrong. We have to do something right. We can't just follow the rules. We have to follow Jesus.

The story of the Rich Young Ruler is one of the saddest stories in the Bible. He could have leveraged his resources, his network, and his energy for kingdom causes, but he spent it all on himself. It reveals that our *greatest asset* becomes our *greatest liability* if we don't use it for God's purposes!

The Rich Young Ruler eventually became the Old Rich Ruler. I don't know what fired across his synapses as he lay on his deathbed, but I have a hunch. It was the moment Jesus said, "Follow me." Those words echoed in his ear until the day he died.

The importance of going all in is best encapsulated in the parable of the bags of gold. The man who got one bag buried it in the ground. He ultimately gave back to the master exactly what the master had given him. And to be perfectly honest, that's not half bad in a recession. He broke even. Yet Jesus called him *wicked*.

That seems like a little bit of an overreaction, doesn't it?

But when I think Jesus is wrong, it reveals something wrong with me—usually a wrong priority or a wrong perspective. The man who buried his bag of gold wasn't willing to gamble on God. And that's the point of this parable: faith is pushing all of your chips to the middle of the table. And that's what Jesus challenged the Rich Young Ruler to do.

> *"If you want to be perfect, go, sell your possessions and give to the poor, and you will have treasure in heaven. Then come, follow me."*

ACCUMULATE EXPERIENCES

Have you ever felt bad for the Rich Young Ruler? Part of me feels like Jesus was asking for too much. *Are You sure You want to ask for everything? Why don't You start with the tithe?* But Jesus goes for the jugular. He asks the Rich Young Ruler to ante up everything. He loved the Rich Young Ruler too much to ask for anything less!

If you feel bad for the Rich Young Ruler, it shouldn't be because of what Jesus asked him to give up. It should be because of the opportunity he passed up. What Jesus asked him to give up was nothing compared to what Jesus would have given him in return.

In a day and age when the average person never traveled outside a thirty-mile radius of their home, Jesus sent His disciples to the ends of the earth. These uneducated fishermen, who would have lived their entire lives within a stone's throw of the Sea of Galilee, traveled all over the ancient world and turned it upside down.

Think about their experiences during their three years with Jesus. They went camping, hiking, fishing, and sailing with the Son of God. They had box seats to every sermon Jesus preached and then hung out with Him backstage. They didn't just witness His miracles. They filleted the miraculous catch of fish, fried it, and ate it. Put that on your bucket list. What kind of price tag would you put on walking on water? Or drinking the water that Jesus turned into wine?

The disciples were poor in terms of material possessions, but they accumulated a wealth of experience unparalleled in human history. The Rich Young Ruler forfeited a wealth of experience because he couldn't let go of his possessions.

SENIOR PARTNER

I have a ninety-five-year-old friend named Stanley Tam. More than a half century ago, Stanley legally transferred 51 percent of the shares of his company to God. Stanley started the United States Plastic Corporation with $37 in capital. When he gave his business back to God, annual revenues were less than $200,000.

After reading the parable about the merchant who sold everything to obtain the pearl of great price, Stanley made a decision to divest himself of the rest of his shares, saying, "A man can eat only one meal at a time, wear only one suit of clothes at a time, drive only one car at a time. All this I have. Isn't that enough?"

On January 15, 1955, every share of stock was transferred to his Senior Partner, and Stanley became a salaried employee of the company he had started. From that day to the present, Stanley has given away more than $120 million!

Is Jesus Christ your Pearl of Great Price?
Is He your Senior Partner?

DRAW THE LINE

Destiny is not a mystery. It's a decision. And you are only one decision away from a totally different life. One decision can totally change your financial forecast. One decision can radically alter a relationship. One decision can lead toward health—spiritual, physical, or emotional. And those defining decisions will become the defining moments of your life.

For Stanley Tam, the defining moment was January 15, 1955.

For me, it was the first day of my sophomore year of college. And there have been a half dozen defining decisions since then. The day we packed all of our earthly belongings into a U-Haul truck and moved to Washington, DC, with no guaranteed salary and no place to live. The day National Community Church decided to launch its second location without knowing where it would be. The day Lora and I made a faith promise to missions that was way beyond our budget.

Those defining decisions proved to be defining moments. You only make a few defining decisions in your life, but they will define your life.

What risk do you need to take?

What sacrifice do you need to make?

This isn't a book to read. It is a decision to be made. If you read this book without making a defining decision, I wasted my time writing it and you wasted your time reading it. At some point, on some page, you will feel the Holy Spirit prompting you to act decisively. Don't ignore it. Obey it.

You need to put Isaac on the altar like Abraham.

You need to throw down your staff like Moses.

You need to burn your plowing equipment like Elisha.

You need to climb the cliff like Jonathan.

You need to get out of the boat like Peter.

There comes a moment when you throw caution to the wind.

There comes a moment when you need to go all in.

This is that moment.

This is your moment.

PART TWO

NOT EASY

FOUR

CHARGE

Joshua Chamberlain was a student of theology and a professor of rhetoric, not a soldier. But when duty called, Chamberlain answered. He climbed the ranks to become colonel of the 20th Maine Volunteer Infantry Regiment, Union Army.

On July 2, 1863, Chamberlain and his three-hundred-soldier regiment were all that stood between the Confederates and certain defeat at a battlefield in Gettysburg, Pennsylvania. At 2:30 p.m., the 15th and 47th Alabama infantry regiments of the Confederate army charged, but Chamberlain and his men held their ground. By the last charge, only eighty blues stood standing. Chamberlain himself was knocked down by a bullet that hit his belt buckle, but the thirty-four-year-old schoolteacher got right back up.

It was his date with destiny.

When Sergeant Tozier informed Chamberlain that no reinforcements were coming and his men were down to one round of ammunition per soldier, Chamberlain knew he needed to act. Their lookout, a young boy perched high in a tree on Little Round Top, informed Colonel Chamberlain that the Confederates were forming rank. The rational thing to do at that point, with no ammunition and no reinforcements, would have been to surrender. But Chamberlain wasn't wired that way. In full view of the enemy, Chamberlain climbed onto their barricade of stones and gave a command. He pointed his sword and yelled, "Charge!"

And in what ranks as one of the most improbable victories in military history, eighty Union soldiers captured four thousand Confederates in five minutes flat.

What seemed like a suicide mission saved the Union.

Historians believe that if Chamberlain had not charged, the rebels would have gained the high ground. If the rebels had gained the high ground, there is a good chance they would have won the Battle of Gettysburg. If the rebels had won that battle, the historical consensus is that the Confederates would have won the war. One man's courage saved the day, saved the war, and saved the Union.

That is how the kingdom of God advances. Going all in means leaving safety behind.

THE INABILITY TO DO NOTHING

After the war, Joshua Chamberlain went on to serve as the thirty-second governor of Maine and the president of his alma mater, Bowdoin College. In 1893, thirty years after his act of heroism, he was awarded the Medal of Honor by President Grover Cleveland for "holding his position on the Little Round Top against repeated assaults, and carrying the advance position on the Great Round Top."

In his later years, Chamberlain would reflect back on the war with these words: "I had deep within me the inability to do nothing. I knew I may die, but I also knew that I would not die with a bullet in my back."

The inability to do nothing!

Isn't that the standard Jesus set?

He single-handedly turned the temple upside down and inside out by turning over tables and tossing out money changers. He confronted the Pharisees' hypocrisy. He exorcised an evil spirit from a man possessed by demons. And He stopped a funeral procession in its tracks by raising a boy from the dead.

Jesus was anything but passive. He was the epitome of passion. So regardless of personality type, His followers ought to be the most passionate people on the planet. No fear means defying religious protocol for the sake of God-ordained passions—like the most famous party crasher of all time did, the prostitute who broke open her bottle of perfume to anoint Jesus's feet.

When will we realize that indecision *is* a decision?

When will we come to terms with the fact that inaction *is* an action?

The church was never meant to be a noun. The church was meant to be a verb, an action verb.

Two thousand years ago, Jesus gave the command to charge!

And He's never sounded the retreat.

PLAY OFFENSE

Despite what the old axiom says, opportunity does *not* knock! You need to knock on the door of opportunity. And sometimes you need to knock the door down!

No fear is not taking no for an answer.

It's a sanctified stubborn streak that doesn't allow us to give up!

Joshua Chamberlain said his stubborn streak is what didn't allow him to give up when things looked hopeless. Referring to himself in the third person, Chamberlain said, "Their leader had no real knowledge of warfare or tactics. I was only a stubborn man and that was my greatest advantage in this fight."

No fear means that you don't give up.

No matter how many times you get knocked down, you get back up.

No matter how tough it gets, you don't give up the fight.

Abraham hoped against hope for a son. And when God finally delivered on a twenty-five-year-old promise, Abraham passed the test of all tests by putting Isaac back on the altar.

Is there something you have given up on?

Maybe you need to double back and try again!

I could have given up after one failed church plant, but I refused to retreat. I could have given up on writing after thirteen years of false starts, but I refused to wave the white flag.

Maybe you're tempted right now to give up on your marriage or give up on your kids.

Hang in there.

This too shall pass.

Even if there are no reinforcements and you're out of ammunition, you need to charge the problem, charge the dream, charge the goal.

Quit making excuses! Don't be afraid.

Stop playing defense and start playing offense.

You need to *charge* your marriage.

You need to *charge* your finances.

CHARGE

You need to *charge* your health.
You need to *charge* your addiction.
You need to *charge* your children.
You need to *charge* your goals.
You need to *charge* kingdom causes.
You need to *charge* Jesus.

FIVE

THIS IS ONLY A TEST

Some time later God tested Abraham. He said to him, "Abraham!"

"Here I am," he replied.

Then God said, "Take your son, your only son, whom you love—Isaac—and go to the region of Moriah. Sacrifice him there as a burnt offering on a mountain I will show you."

GENESIS 22:1–2

The story of God calling Abraham to sacrifice Isaac is tough to stomach. How could a loving heavenly Father even suggest such a thing? But the biblical stories that cause the most cognitive dissonance to our logical minds often contain the greatest revelations. Too often we approach stories like this one as if God is on trial, but it's not *His* character that is in question. It's *our* character that is on the stand. And that is precisely why God tests us.

God never intended for Abraham to sacrifice his son. It was only a test. God would not have allowed the slaying of Isaac. He simply wanted to test Abraham to see if he was willing to obey the most counterintuitive command imaginable. Scripture explicitly reads, "God tested Abraham." And Abraham passed the test. That's how you get a testimony. No test = no testimony. So the next time you are tested, recognize it for what it is.

I didn't get a testimony in seminary. I got a great education, but you don't get a testimony by listening to a lecture or sermon or speech in the comfortable confines of a classroom, church, or conference. You get a testimony in the wilderness like Moses, on the Sea of Galilee like Peter, on the mountain like Abraham.

THE PROVING GROUND

According to Jewish tradition, God gave Abraham ten different tests. This one is the final exam. It was brilliantly and specifically designed to test whether or not Abraham was all in.

God tests us for two primary reasons.

First, it's an opportunity for God to prove Himself to us.

Second, it's an opportunity for us to prove ourselves to God.

That's why we should consider it joy when we experience trials. They're the way we graduate to the next grade in God's kingdom. I know some people who have been saved for twenty-five years, but they don't have twenty-five years of experience. They have one year of experience repeated twenty-five times. They are frustrated with their faith, but it's because they aren't learning the lessons God is trying to teach them.

When Abraham raised the knife, God knew that Abraham was all in because he was willing to sacrifice what was most precious to him. And God proved Himself as Provider. If

Abraham had stayed afraid, he would have robbed God of the opportunity to provide a ram in the thicket. But because Abraham had no fear, God was able to reveal Himself as Jehovah-jireh, God our Provider.

When I was in seminary, I tried to plant a church on Chicago's North Shore. I actually created a twenty-five-year plan as part of my master's program. My professor gave it an A, but God gave it an F. It wasn't His plan. It was mine. I went into it for all the wrong reasons. That church plant was my Isaac, and I knew I needed to put it on the altar. When that dream died, God provided a ram in the thicket. One day I was flipping through a magazine and read about a parachurch ministry in Washington, DC. It caught the corner of my eye, just like the ram that came into Abraham's peripheral view. I made a phone call that led to a visit that led to us packing all of our earthly belongings into a U-Haul truck and moving to Washington, DC. We didn't have a place to live or a guaranteed salary. We weren't safe, but we had a resurrected dream.

ID YOUR ISAAC

God will never tempt you. It's not in His nature. He promises to provide an escape route for every tempting situation. But God will test your faith. And those tests will get progressively harder as the stakes get higher. And those tests will revolve around what is most important to you.

What do you find your identity in?

What do you find your security in?

That's your Isaac.

God will test you to make sure your identity and your

security are found in the cross of Jesus Christ. And God will go after anything you trust in more than Him until you put it on the altar.

You don't have to live in fear that God is going to take away what is most important to you. Isaac was God's gift to Abraham. But if the gift ever becomes more important than the Gift Giver, then the very thing God gave you to serve His purposes is undermining His plan for your life. And when God becomes the means to some other end, you have inverted the gospel.

One of my recurrent prayers is this: *Lord, don't let my gifts take me farther than my character can sustain me.* As we cultivate the gifts God has given us, we can begin to rely on those gifts instead of relying on God.

It was God who gave Lucifer a beautiful form and a beautiful voice. Those gifts were originally used to glorify God. Then Lucifer started looking in the mirror, started reflecting on his own beauty. He glorified the gift he had been given instead of glorifying God. The lesson of Lucifer's fall is this: *whatever you don't turn into praise turns into pride.*

What are your greatest God-given gifts?

What are your most significant God-ordained opportunities?

What God-sized dreams has the Holy Spirit conceived in your spirit?

That's your Isaac.

THE DEATH OF A DREAM

A few years ago, I met Phil Vischer, the creator of VeggieTales. Phil started out with loose change and a God-idea called Big Idea, Inc. The company sold more than fifty million videos and grossed hundreds of millions of dollars, but it all ended with one lawsuit. As Phil himself said, "Fourteen years' worth of work flashed before my eyes—the characters, the songs, the impact, the letters from kids all over the world. It all flashed before my eyes, then it all vanished."

Big Idea declared bankruptcy, and the dream died a painful death. That's when Phil heard a sermon that saved his soul.

> If God gives you a dream, and the dream comes to life and God shows up in it, and then the dream dies, it may be that God wants to see what is more important to you—the dream or him.

Which do you love more: the dream God gave to you or the God who gave you the dream?

Every dream I've ever had has gone through a death and a resurrection. The dream of planting a church had to die so it could be resurrected in glorified form. By glorified form, I simply mean doing it for God's glory.

If your God-ordained dream becomes more important to you than God, you have to put it on the altar and raise the knife. And once the dream is dead and buried, it can be resurrected for God's glory.

The Holy Spirit is the Dream Maker. Just as He hovered over the chaos at the dawn of creation, He overshadows all creation. If you're walking in lockstep with the Holy Spirit, He will conceive a single-cell desire within you that has the potential to become a God-sized dream if nurtured with prayer.

I'd rather have one God-idea than a thousand good ideas. Good ideas are good, but God-ideas change the course of history. You can get good ideas in a lot of different places—classrooms, conferences, and bookstores. But God-ideas only come from one place—the Holy Spirit Himself.

Isaac was God's idea. It was God who proclaimed the promise to Abraham and conceived the promise within Sarah. Postmenopausal octogenarians don't get pregnant. Period. But God always delivers what He conceives if we are willing to go through the labor pains.

MY ISAAC

The church ought to be the most creative place on the planet. There are ways of doing church that no one has thought of yet. That driving motivation is what gets me up early and keeps me up late. And I believe that my passion to do church differently was put there by the Holy Spirit. I have no doubt that God is the one who called me and gifted me to serve as lead pastor of National Community Church, but it also means NCC is my Isaac.

I wouldn't want to be anyplace else doing anything else. I've invested sixteen years of blood, sweat, and tears into this God-ordained dream called National Community Church, and I pray for the privilege of serving there for the rest of my life. I absolutely love what I do. But if I love it more than I love God, then the very thing God has called me to do is no longer serving His purposes.

I never use the possessive pronoun *my* when referring to National Community Church. I love it when NCCers refer to NCC as their church, but I'm careful not to. Christ is the Shepherd. As pastor, I'm the undershepherd. I always want to remember it's not *my* church. It's *His* church. It's a gift from God and for God.

The truth of the matter is that you can't really say *mine* about anything! Nothing belongs to you—not your house, not your car, not your clothes. Every material thing you own is the by-product of the time, talent, and treasure God has given you.

When you kneel at the foot of the cross, the possessive pronoun is eliminated from your vocabulary.

There is no more *me*, *my*, or *mine*.

The early Methodists devoted themselves entirely to God with a covenant prayer:

> I am no longer my own, but Thine. Put me to what Thou wilt, rank me with whom Thou wilt; put me to doing, put me to suffering; let me be employed for Thee or laid aside for Thee, exalted for Thee or brought low for thee; let me be full, let me be empty; let me have all things, let me have nothing; I freely and heartily yield all things to Thy pleasure and disposal.
>
> And now, O glorious and blessed God, Father, Son, and Holy Spirit, Thou art mine, and I am Thine. So be it. And the covenant, which I have made on earth, let it be ratified in heaven. Amen.

WHOSE YOU ARE

Do you find your identity in *who you are* or *whose you are*?

You can base your identity on a thousand things—the degrees you've earned, the positions you hold, the salary you make, the trophies you've won, the hobbies you have, the way you look, the way you dress, or even the car you drive. But if you base your identity on any of those temporal things, your identity is a house of cards. There is only one solid foundation: Jesus Christ. If you find security in *what you have done*, you will always fall short of the righteous standard set by the sinless Son of God. There is only one place in which to find your true identity and eternal security: *what Christ has done for you*.

Religion is spelled *do*.

The gospel is spelled *done*.

Going all in means 100 percent reliance on the atoning work of Christ. It's not 99 percent grace and 1 percent good works. The problem is that most of us still want 1 percent credit for the things we've done right, but it's *all* grace or *no* grace. There is no partial credit. You are not part of the equation of salvation. You cannot trust Jesus Christ 99 percent. Trust is a 100 percent proposition.

It's addition by subtraction.

So the question is this: What do you need to give up? What do you need to put on the altar? Where do you find your security outside of Christ?

PUT IT ON THE ALTAR

The harder you have to work for something, the harder it is to give it up. And the longer you have to wait for it, the tougher it is to give it back. Isaac was the lifelong dream of a barren woman named Sarah and an impotent man named Abraham. Isaac was the promise they white-knuckled for twenty-five years!

The more God blesses you, the harder it is to keep that blessing from becoming an idol in your life. Money may be the best example. The more money you make, the harder it is to trust Almighty God and the easier it is to trust the Almighty Dollar. Isn't it ironic that "In God We Trust" is printed on the very thing we find it most difficult to trust God with?

Our tendency is to object to all-in assertions with loopholes. *Shouldn't I save for retirement? Doesn't the Bible tell me to leave an inheritance? Don't I need to provide for my family's welfare?* I'm not saying we shouldn't do any of those things. But that doesn't keep me from asking the point-blank question: Are you willing to give it all away?

SIX

BURN THE SHIPS

So Elisha left him and went back. He took his yoke of oxen and slaughtered them. He burned the plowing equipment to cook the meat and gave it to the people, and they ate. Then he set out to follow Elijah and became his servant.

1 KINGS 19:21

On February 19, 1519, the Spanish explorer Hernán Cortés set sail for Mexico with an entourage of 11 ships, 13 horses, 110 sailors, and 553 soldiers. The indigenous population upon his arrival was approximately five million. From a purely mathematical standpoint, the odds were stacked against him by a ratio of 7,541 to 1.

After landing, He issued an order that turned his mission into an all-or-nothing proposition: *Burn the ships!* If you can compartmentalize the moral conundrum of colonization, there is a lesson to be learned. Nine times out of ten, failure is resorting to Plan B when Plan A gets too risky, too costly, or too difficult. That's why most people are living their Plan B. They didn't burn the ships. Plan A people don't have a Plan B.

They would rather crash and burn going after their God-ordained dreams than succeed at something else.

There are moments in life when we need to burn the ships to our past. You burn the ships named *Past Failure* and *Past Success*. You burn the ship named *Bad Habit*. You burn the ship named *Regret*. You burn the ship named *Guilt*. You burn the ship named *My Old Way of Life*.

That is precisely what Elisha did when he turned his plowing equipment into kindling and barbequed his oxen. It was his last supper. He said good-bye to his old life by throwing a party for his friends. They shared a meal and shared stories into the early-morning hours. But it was the bonfire that made it the most meaningful and memorable night of his life because it symbolized the old Elisha. It was the last day of his old life and the first day of his new life.

Burning the plowing equipment was Elisha's way of burning the ships. He couldn't go back to his old way of life because he destroyed the time machine that would take him back. It was the end of Elisha the farmer. It was the beginning of Elisha the prophet.

Stop and think about the symbolism of what Elisha did. Elisha literally cooked his old way of life and ate it for dinner. He eliminated the possibility of going back to farming by eating his own oxen and burning his plowing equipment.

It doesn't matter whether you're trying to lose weight, get into graduate school, write a book, start a business, or get out of debt. The first step is always the longest and the hardest. And you can't just take a step forward into the future. You also have to eliminate the possibility of moving backward into the past.

That's how you go after goals.

That's how you break addictions.

That's how you reconcile relationships.

You leave the past in the past by burning the ships.

A NEW CHAPTER

In order to begin a new chapter, you must end an old chapter. The way to do it is with a simple punctuation mark. You can put a period on the page. But if you want to be more dramatic, you can use an exclamation point. It's more decisive, more definitive. Then you turn the page and begin a new sentence, which begins a new paragraph, which begins a new chapter.

What's true in grammar is true in life.

Elisha didn't need to burn his plowing equipment to follow Elijah, but it made a statement. More specifically, it was a statement of faith. There was no turning back. If his prophetic apprenticeship with Elijah didn't pan out, he had no place else to turn.

This was Elisha's no-fear moment. Elisha wasn't just buying in. He was selling out. And that's what going *all in* is all about. It's being fully present in the here and now. It's not living past tense or future tense. That doesn't mean you don't learn from the past or plan for the future, but you don't live there. Going all in is living as though each day is the first day and last day of your life.

Have you made a statement of faith?

I'm not talking about repeating a sinner's prayer or taking a confirmation class. A statement of faith must make a statement. It's a defining decision accompanied by a dramatic action that symbolizes your absolute commitment to Jesus Christ and His cause.

Think about it.
Pray about it.
Then act on it.

MAKE A STATEMENT

Michael and Maria Durso are the founders of Christ Tabernacle in Queens, New York. In their twenties, Michael and Maria were as far from God as you can get. They were living together, from drug fix to drug fix. Then one day Maria mysteriously came under the conviction of the Holy Spirit. She wasn't in church. She wasn't reading a Bible. She was in their hotel room on vacation when the conviction came out of nowhere. What she didn't know until she returned home is that a group of her friends had gotten saved while she was away. At that very moment, thousands of miles away, they were forming a prayer circle and interceding for Maria.

When they returned to New York, Michael and Maria stopped sleeping together and started going to church together. After making the decision to follow Christ, Michael knew he needed to divorce himself from his past. He gathered all of his drug paraphernalia, along with magazines and videos that were vestiges of his old self. One by one, he dropped them down the incinerator chute of their New York City apartment building.

That's a statement of faith.

Please make no mistake. We are saved by grace through faith. You are not more saved or less saved based on how creative or compelling or courageous your statement of faith is. It's all about the cross of Jesus Christ. But a statement of faith makes it personal, makes it memorable.

Remember the tax collector who put his faith in Christ?

He gave half of his possessions to the poor. That isn't what saved him. But that dramatic action was evidence of a defining decision! He also offered to pay back four times as much to anyone he had cheated. Before he met Jesus, money was his god. So it makes sense that his statement of faith would involve finances.

Remember the prostitute who anointed Jesus?

She broke open her alabaster jar. That isn't what saved her. But that dramatic action was evidence of a defining decision! She gave her most precious possession to Jesus. Breaking it open was her way of burning the plowing equipment. She was giving up her former life by giving that jar to Jesus.

Remember the revival that broke out in Ephesus?

Those who practiced sorcery burned their scrolls publicly. The cumulative value of those scrolls was estimated at fifty thousand drachmas. A drachma was a silver coin worth a day's wages. That's 138 years of wages! They made a $3,739,972.50 statement of faith.

PAST TENSE

We want God to do something new while we keep doing the same old thing. We want God to change our circumstances without us having to change at all. But if we are asking God for new wine, we will need a new wineskin.

Change is a two-sided coin.

Out with the old is one side.

In with the new is the other side.

Most of us get stuck spiritually because we keep doing the

same thing while expecting different results. What got you to where you are may not get you to where God wants you to go next.

> *Seek me and live;*
> *do not seek Bethel,*
> *do not go to Gilgal,*
> *do not journey to Beersheba ...*
> *Seek the LORD and live.*

Bethel is the place where Jacob had his life-changing dream. He built an altar and made a vow. Gilgal is the place where the Israelites camped after God miraculously parted the Jordan River and they stepped foot into the Promised Land for the first time. It only took one night to get Israel out of Egypt, but it took forty years to get Egypt out of Israel. Gilgal marks the spot where God rolled away their reproach. Beersheba is the place where Abraham made a treaty with Abimelek and called on the Lord. His son Isaac dug a well and built an altar there.

All three places held special significance. They were sacred landmarks in Israel's spiritual journey. So why would God tell them *not* to seek Him there? Because you won't find God in the past. His name is not *I WAS*. His name is *I AM*. He is an *ever-present* help. And when we cling too tightly to what God did last, we often miss what God wants to do next.

PRESS ON

At some point in our lives, most of us stop living out of imagination and start living out of memory. That's the day we stop living and start dying. And that's the impetus behind Paul's exhortation in Philippians 3:13–14:

> *Forgetting what is behind and straining toward what is ahead, I press on toward the goal to win the prize for which God has called me heavenward in Christ Jesus.*

I love that little phrase: *press on.*

Whenever I hear it, I have flashbacks to my college basketball days. There are two ways of playing defense. You can sit back in a half-court defense and let the other team come to you. Then there is an offensive form of defense—the full-court press. You force the issue. You don't let the game come to you. You take it to them.

I wonder if the church is content playing half-court defense while God is calling for a full-court press. Isn't that the message of Matthew 11:12?

> *"From the days of John the Baptist until now, the kingdom of heaven has been forcefully advancing, and forceful men lay hold of it."*

Are you playing offense in your marriage? Or are you playing a defense that leaves romance on the sidelines? Are you parenting reactively or proactively? Do you have a spiritual growth plan? Are you working for a paycheck or stewarding your God-given gifts pursuing a God-ordained dream? Are you trying to break even spiritually by avoiding sin? Or are you going for broke by invading the darkness with the light and love of Jesus Christ?

At the end of every year, Lora and I take a little retreat

to reflect on the past year and plan for the next one. The top priorities are calendar and budget. If we don't control our calendar, our calendar will end up controlling us. Budgeting is the way we play offense with our finances. I also revisit my life goal list and set spiritual goals for the next calendar year. Then on Mondays, which is my Sabbath, Lora and I do a coffee date. It's a weekly touch point to make sure we're working the plan with our family and our finances. The only way to predict the future is to create it. You don't let it happen. You make it happen. How? Stop regretting the past and start learning from it. Let go of guilt by leaning into God's grace. Quit beating yourself up and let the Spirit of God heal your heart. God wants to reconcile your past by redeeming it.

The spiritual tipping point is when the pain of staying the same becomes greater than the pain of change. Too many of us get comfortable with comfort. We follow Christ to the point of inconvenience, but no further. That's when we need a prophet to walk into our lives, throw a mantle around our shoulders, and wake us up to a new possibility, a new reality. We need a prophet to boldly confront Plan B and call us back to Plan A.

DANCING MEADOW

Elisha was born and raised in a region of Israel known as Abel Meholah, or the "meadow of dancing." It was the breadbasket of the Jordan River valley. And Elisha's family had a profitable farming operation. Most family farms were small enterprises consisting of a single plow with one set of oxen. Having twelve yoke of oxen, along with the farmhands to plow with them, is evidence that Elisha came from wealth. Burning the plowing equipment was more than quitting his job. It meant divesting himself of his share in the family. It may have even been writing himself out of the family will.

We tend to hedge our bets. Not Elisha. He wasn't 100 percent committed to Elijah. Elisha was 200 percent committed. And that's what gave him the boldness to ask for a double portion of Elijah's anointing. And God granted it. During his sixty years of prophetic ministry, Elisha performed twenty-eight miracles as recorded in Scripture. That's twice as many as the fourteen miracles that the prophet Elijah performed.

What gave Elisha the holy boldness to ask for a double portion? Elisha didn't withhold anything from God. And if you give all of yourself to God, you can ask and expect that God will give all of Himself to you because that's precisely what He wants to do. We have not because we ask not, and we ask not because we're staying safe!

Elisha could have lived his entire life in the dancing meadow. So can you. You can keep plowing your fields instead of following the call of God, but you might very well be forfeiting twenty-eight miracles.

DOUBLE ANOINTING

I was sitting in a Doctor of Ministry class at Regent University when a school administrator interrupted the class and told me my wife needed to speak to me.

"Mark, my dad died." It was the most shocking moment of my life.

My father-in-law was in the prime of life, the prime of ministry. Two days before his death, he'd had his annual physical, and the doctor had said, "You could drive a Mack Truck through your arteries." So how could he die of a massive heart attack forty-eight hours later?

We drove from Virginia Beach to DC in record time. Then we caught a flight to Chicago, where we met the rest of our family at the funeral home that evening. To see his body in a casket was like a bad dream, but one from which we'd never wake up.

My father-in-law, Bob Schmidgall, was my ministry hero. He was a ten-talent leader and teacher. I've never met anybody who prayed with more intensity, more consistency. At the time of his death, he was pastoring the same church he had started in 1967 with my mother-in-law. It was one of the largest and most generous churches in the country, giving millions of dollars to missions. By comparison, I was pastoring a new church plant with very few people and very little money. It didn't even feel like a church, and I didn't feel like a pastor. As I stood by the casket, I felt prompted by the Holy Spirit to ask God for a double portion of my father-in-law's anointing. I didn't know exactly what that meant. I just knew I wanted his legacy to live on in me the way Elijah's legacy lived on in Elisha. And I think it does. The church I pastor is still not as large as the church my father-in-law planted, but we have the same heartbeat. National Community Church will take twenty-five mission trips and give more than $2 million to missions this year.

The anointing is difficult to define, but here's my take. The anointing is the difference between *what you can do* and *what God can do*. It's the difference between the temporal and the eternal. It's the difference between success and failure.

BACK TO THE BEGINNING

It's tough to rank the prophets, but if there were an ancient fantasy league in Israel, Elisha would be a first-round pick. Every miracle is miraculous. But Elisha gets extra credit for parting the Jordan River, raising a boy from the dead, and making an iron axhead float.

So why did God give Elisha a double portion?

He asked for it. Elisha didn't hold out on God, so God didn't hold out on Elisha. Elisha had no fear.

Burning the plowing equipment was handing in his resignation as CEO of Elisha Farms, Inc. And Elisha gave it up for an unpaid internship with an itinerant prophet named Elijah. He went from the very top of the totem pole to the very bottom. As an intern, he got the jobs no one else wanted to do. You have to be willing to climb the ladder, starting with the bottom rung.

Every black belt had to start as a white belt.

Every concert pianist started out with scales.

Every PhD started out in kindergarten.

If you aren't willing to begin at the beginning, God cannot use you. You've got to be willing to be demoted from first to last. Isn't that the example Jesus set? The all-powerful Creator became a servant.

Are you willing to start all over again? Empty your savings account? Give someone a second chance? Make the move?

We have a protégé program at National Community Church. It's a one-year unpaid internship, and protégés have to raise their own support to come. But if they are willing to make the financial sacrifice, they will get a once-in-a-lifetime experience.

Heather Zempel leads our small group ministry at National Community Church. I've never met anybody more passionate about spiritual formation. A decade ago, Heather was working on Capitol Hill for a United States senator. She was willing to give up the prestige of working on Capitol Hill and all the perks that come with it to start all over again as a protégé. She burned her ships. We only had two small groups at the time, but over the past decade she has raised up hundreds of leaders. She has engineered our system of small groups that meet seven days a week all over the DC metro area. That's how every success story begins in the kingdom of God. In God's upside-down kingdom, a step down is a step up. And if you're willing to be demoted in the eyes of man, then you're ready to be promoted by God Himself.

It's difficult to imagine burning our ships, because we can't see any other way across the Jordan River. But if we have the courage to burn the ships, God will part the river. And we'll discover that we didn't need them to get where God wants us to go. God Himself will get us there. And God Himself will get the glory!

SEVEN

CRASH THE PARTY

When one of the Pharisees invited Jesus to have dinner with him, he went to the Pharisee's house and reclined at the table. A woman in that town who lived a sinful life learned that Jesus was eating at the Pharisee's house, so she came there with an alabaster jar of perfume. As she stood behind him at his feet weeping, she began to wet his feet with her tears. Then she wiped them with her hair, kissed them and poured perfume on them.

LUKE 7:36–38

When you read the Bible, don't check your sense of humor at the door. A party hosted by a Pharisee? That's downright funny! If ever there was an oxymoron, it has to be *Pharisee party*. Come on, how fun could it have been? No deejay. No punch. And definitely no pigs in blankets because that wouldn't have been kosher!

Then in walks this woman.

The Pharisees blushed, but I bet Jesus had a twinkle in His eye. He knew it was about to get as fun as doing some healing on the Sabbath. For the record, Jesus could have healed on any day of the week. I think He deliberately chose the Sabbath because it'd be far more fun if He riled up a few religious folks along the way. And if you follow in His footsteps, you'll offend some Pharisees as well.

Can you imagine the look on the Pharisees' straitlaced faces when this woman makes her surprise appearance? They start coughing uncontrollably when she breaks open her alabaster jar of perfume. And then she starts wiping Jesus's feet with her hair.

Can you say *awkward*?

But she made a statement, didn't she?

This act of worship ranks as one of the most beautiful and meaningful statements of faith in all of Scripture. She risked her reputation—what little she had left of it—to anoint Jesus. She knew the Pharisees stoned women like her, but she didn't stay safe. She used her most precious possession—an alabaster jar of perfume—to make her profession of faith.

BREAK THE ALABASTER JAR

The alabaster jar of perfume was pure nard, a perennial herb that is harvested in the Himalayas. Half a liter of it, no less! And the jar itself, made of semitransparent gemstones, was probably a family heirloom. It might have even been her dowry.

The alabaster jar represented her past guilt and future hope. It represented both her professional identity and financial security. How ironic, yet how appropriate, that the perfume used in her profession as a prostitute would become the token of her profession of faith. She anted up by pouring out every last drop at the feet of Jesus.

Breaking that bottle was her way of burning the ships. She walked out of the dark shadow of sin and into the light of the world.

There comes a moment when we need to come clean.

There comes a moment when we need to unveil the secret shame of sin.

There comes a moment when we need to fall full-weight on the grace of God.

This is that moment for this woman.

Why do we act as though our sin disqualifies us from the grace of God? That is the *only* thing that qualifies us! Anything else is a self-righteous attempt to earn God's grace. You cannot trust God's grace 99 percent. It's all or nothing. The problem is that we want partial credit for our salvation. We want to be 1 percent of the equation. But if we try to save ourselves, we forfeit the salvation that comes from Jesus Christ alone, by grace through faith.

Going all in means radical repentance. Put all of your cards face up on the table via confession. A half-hearted confession of sin always results in a half-hearted love for Christ. Downplaying sin is downplaying grace. And it dishonors the sacrifice of the Sinless One.

What would happen if we mustered the moral courage of this woman, walked into a room full of self-righteous Pharisees, and revealed our sin unashamedly while anointing Jesus as Lord and Savior?

I know exactly what would happen: a revival on earth and a party in heaven.

SPIRITUAL DOWRY

The alabaster jar ranks as one of the most unique offerings in Scripture. It was an intimate expression of love, an extravagant expression of faith.

Our church recently received a gift that falls in that same category.

The pain in Shelley's heart was written all over her face. The dream of marriage had turned into a nightmare when her fiancé unexpectedly and inexplicably broke off their engagement. Shelley felt like there was no way out of the prison of bitterness she found herself in. And it felt like solitary confinement. That's when she felt prompted to give away what had once been her most precious possession—her engagement ring. She literally handed me the ring box and said, "God told me to give this to the church."

It was Shelley's statement of faith.

Then she preached a one-sentence sermon. She said, "I believe my act of obedience can turn into someone else's miracle."

And it did.

When Matt started attending National Community Church with his girlfriend, Jessica, he realized he had never defined his relationship with God. He wanted all the benefits without any of the commitment. And the same was true of his relationship with Jessica. As Matt got more engaged at NCC, some Elijahs came into his life to call him out of his sin and into the grace of God. When Matt confessed his addiction to pornography, it was a brand-new beginning. Confession breaks the power of canceled sin. Matt left fear behind. He meant business, and that meant reestablishing biblical boundaries in his life. Moving out of the apartment he shared with Jess was a step forward spiritually, but it was a step backward financially.

Matt wanted nothing more than to propose to Jess, but he felt he needed to save enough money to buy a ring first. As soon as he saved any money, an unexpected financial emergency would drain his savings. It was right about the time that Matt was giving up on getting a ring for Jessica that Shelley gave her ring to NCC. We started praying that God would reveal the ones to whom the ring belonged, and it became evident that Matt's and Jessica's names were all over it.

Not long after we surprised Matt with the ring, he surprised Jessica. Matt pulled out the little black box while paddleboating on the Tidal Basin. He actually had a string tied to it because he was afraid he'd drop it in the water because he'd be shaking so bad! Matt managed to get down on one knee, which is no easy accomplishment in a paddleboat, and pop the question. Shelley's obedience turned into Matt and Jessica's miracle!

One footnote.

Before Matt popped the question, he asked Jessica's dad if he could ask for his daughter's hand in marriage. Matt's father-in-law said, "All I've ever wanted for my children is that they would marry someone who loves Jesus first and foremost." Then he put Matt on the spot: "Matthew, can you tell me that you love Jesus more than Jessica?" Matt paused for a moment and then said, "For the first time in my life, I can honestly say yes!"

What is most precious to you?

Your spouse? Your children? Your job? Your paycheck? Your past accomplishments? Your future goals?

That is your alabaster jar of perfume.

Do you love Jesus more than your most precious possession? The most precious person in your life? Your deepest desire? Your greatest goal? Your proudest accomplishment?

Do you love Jesus first? Or second? Or third? Or tenth?

BRASS TACKS

It's quite possible that the alabaster jar of perfume represented every penny of this woman's life savings. Two gospel writers find it noteworthy enough to give us a written estimate: three hundred denarii—the equivalent of an entire year's salary!

Let's get down to brass tacks.

For most of us, the alabaster jar of perfume is money. It's our nest egg. It's our paycheck, our stock portfolio, and our 401(k). And the question is this: Are you willing to give it all away? I'm not suggesting you should not pay your bills or plan for your future or take care of your family. But if the Holy Spirit prompted you to give it all away, would you be willing to break open your alabaster jar and pour it all—every last drop—at the feet of Jesus?

Let me be blunt, because on the subject of money Jesus was. Obedience can be measured in *dollars*. So can faith. So can sacrifice. It's certainly not the *only* measure, but it's one of the most accurate. If we give God 2 percent of our income, can we really say we are 100 percent committed to Him? If we withhold the tithe, can we really say, "In God we trust"? If we give God our leftovers instead of the firstfruits, can we really say we're seeking first His kingdom? God doesn't need our money, but He does want our heart. When we give money to a kingdom cause, we aren't giving money. We are giving part of ourselves. We traded our time and talent for that money. That gift, just like the alabaster jar of perfume, is an intimate expression of who we are.

STANDARD OF GIVING

John Wesley is most famous for circuit riding, open-air preaching, and the Methodist movement. But Wesley was an even better giver than he was a preacher! He lived by a simple maxim: *Make all you can. Save all you can. Give all you can.*

Our family has adopted that maxim as our own. Every year we try to increase the percentage of income we give away. During his lifetime, Wesley gave away approximately 30,000 pounds. Adjusted for inflation, that would equate to $1,764,705.88 in today's dollars!

The genesis of Wesley's generosity was a covenant he made with God in 1731. He decided to limit his expenses so he had more margin to give. His income ceiling was 28 pounds. That first year, John Wesley only made 30 pounds, so he gave just 2 pounds. The next year, his income doubled, and because he managed to continue living on 28 pounds, he had 32 pounds to give away! In the third year, his income increased to 90 pounds, but he kept his expenses flat.

Wesley's goal was to give away all excess income after bills were paid and family needs were taken care of. He believed that God's blessings should result in us raising not our *standard of living* but our *standard of giving*.

Wesley continued to raise his standard of giving. Even when his income rose into the thousands of pounds, he lived simply and gave away all surplus money. He died with a few coins in his pocket but a storehouse of treasure in heaven. When it came to his financial needs, Wesley left safety up to God.

A BEAUTIFUL THING

Our reactions reveal more about us than our actions. And the reaction of the disciples is telling when the woman broke open the alabaster jar. "Why this waste?" They thought this woman was pouring this perfume down the drain by pouring it at Jesus's feet. They were offended by it. Jesus defended it. What they called a *waste* He called *a beautiful thing*:

> *"Wherever this gospel is preached throughout the world, what she has done will also be told, in memory of her."*

Can you imagine what this one statement did for her self-image? I bet it had been years since she'd heard a kind word or a compliment. This one sentence punctuated her life. It ended the old chapter and began a new one.

Jesus wasn't predicting fifteen minutes of fame. He was prophesying that she would make His name famous all around the world for all time by her one act of sacrifice! For this one courageous act! What are the odds?

I'm not sure where you are reading right now, but you are fulfilling his prophecy. From Kennebunkport, Maine, to San Diego, California. From the Florida Keys to International Falls, Minnesota. From Brazil to Indonesia to Russia to Korea to Ireland. No one can spot potential like Jesus. Potential is God's gift to us. What we do with it is our gift back to God.

LIVE UP TO

Jesus gave this woman *something to live up to*. That's what prophets do! And that's the exact opposite of what the Pharisees did. They murmured to each other, "If this man were a prophet, he would know who is touching him and what kind of woman she is—that she is a sinner."

The only thing the Pharisees saw when they looked at this woman was a sinner.

I think Jesus saw an innocent little girl playing with her favorite doll—a little girl who had hopes and dreams that were nothing like the reality she was living. He sees past the past. He sees past the sin. He sees His image in us. Like looking in a mirror, God sees a reflection of Himself.

Pharisees treat people based on past performance.

Prophets treat people based on future potential.

Pharisees give people something to live down to.

Prophets give people something to live up to.

Pharisees write people off.

Prophets write people in.

Pharisees see sin.

Prophets see the image of God.

Pharisees give up on people.

Prophets give them a second chance.

The Pharisees reduced this woman to a label—sinner. And we do the same. We give people political labels, sexual labels, and religious labels. But in the process, we strip them of their individuality and complexity. Jesus is in the business of turning bad beginnings into *happily ever afters*.

He did it for the woman caught in the act of adultery.

He did it for the thief on the cross.

And He'll do it for you.

God cannot give up on you. It's not in His nature. His goodness and mercy will follow you all the days of your life. All you have to do is turn around. All you have to do is crash the party!

DESPERADOS

This prostitute was *not* on the guest list. But she was very good at getting in and out of back doors. There would have been safer times or safer places to anoint Jesus, but she decided to crash the party.

Jesus didn't have the time of day for religiosity. Religious protocol meant nothing to Him. If it did, He would have chosen the Pharisees as His disciples. Jesus loved, praised, and rewarded one thing: *desperation for God that superseded decorum*. Jesus loved spiritual desperados.

Jesus honored the tax collector who climbed a sycamore tree in his three-piece suit just to get a glimpse of Jesus by having lunch with him. Jesus honored the woman who fought her way through the crowds just to touch the hem of His garment by healing her chronic illness. And Jesus honored this prostitute who crashed the party by restoring her dignity and giving her a new lease on life.

Nothing has changed.

God is still honoring desperados who climb trees, fight crowds, and crash parties.

How desperate are you?

Desperate enough to make a move, make a change, make a sacrifice?

Desperate enough to pray through the night? Read through the Bible? Reconcile a conflict? Plead with a friend who is a lost soul? Give your life savings to a kingdom cause?

Desperate enough to go all in with God?

True spirituality is "the place where desperation meets Jesus."

Don't be afraid.

Crash the party!

PART THREE

NOT HALFWAY

EIGHT

RIM HUGGERS

Of all the life goals I've achieved, hiking the Grand Canyon from rim to rim with my son, Parker, ranks right at the top of the list. We left safe and comfortable at the rim of the canyon. I don't think I've ever done anything more physically demanding, but that is what made it so memorable.

My first glimpse of the Grand Canyon through the picture window at the Grand Canyon Lodge was unforgettable. I stood and stared for an hour. To simply call the Grand Canyon one of the seven natural wonders of the world seems like geological and theological blasphemy. Magnum opus is more like it. When the sunrise paints the western wall in pink and purple hues, it's like seeing the Creator's reflection.

I've hiked the Inca Trail and climbed Half Dome, but those challenges weren't nearly as difficult or dangerous as crossing 23.2 miles of canyon in two days, with a one-mile descent and ascent in elevation. And we did it in 110-degree temperatures! I lost thirteen pounds in two days!

My primary concern was the safety of my twelve-year-old son. I thought we had more than enough water in our packs, but we ran out and cramped up three miles before reaching our day-one destination. I kept monitoring Parker, "How are you doing on a scale of 1 to 10?" The number kept dropping until he said, "Negative one!"

When we arrived at Phantom Ranch on the canyon floor around dusk, we felt like a car rolling into a gas station on fumes. We had just enough energy to eat dinner and collapse into bed. When my alarm went off at four-thirty the next morning, I felt paralyzed. We chose the shorter yet steeper route out of the canyon with dozens of switchbacks on the final leg. We chose poorly!

As we zigzagged our way up, we could see hundreds of sightseers lining the South Rim. They were as mesmerized by its majesty as we had been the day before. And that's when the contrast struck me. Our clothes were caked with orange-colored canyon clay mixed with salty sweat stains. Flies hovered. The sightseers who lined the rim looked like they had just picked up their neatly pressed clothes at the cleaners. We were absolutely parched and scorched. They looked like they had just emerged from their air-conditioned hotel rooms after a cool shower. Some of them were licking ice cream cones.

For a split second, I felt sorry for myself. Then I felt sorry for them. They were *seeing it* and *missing it* at the same time. That's when I came up with a name for the people who stand and stare, but never hike into the canyon.

Rim huggers.

When Parker and I reached the South Rim, the first thing we did was turn around and look at the trail we had traversed. We stood right next to rim huggers with the very same view, but they didn't appreciate it like we did. They were *seeing* it secondhand, but we had *experienced* it firsthand. I'm sure some of those rim huggers knew some things about the canyon that I didn't—facts they'd read in a travel guide or park brochure. So I guess you could say they knew more about the canyon than we did, but it was nothing more than head knowledge. Hikers know the canyon in a way that huggers never will. Huggers may talk the talk, but hikers walk the walk.

There is a world of difference between *knowing about God* and *knowing God*. The difference between those two things is the distance between the North Rim and South Rim, with the canyon in between.

Most Christians are rim huggers!

WE DON'T GET CREDIT
FOR AN AUDIT

We all want to spend *eternity* with God. We just don't want to spend *time* with Him. We stand and stare from a distance, satisfied with superficiality. We Facebook more than we seek His face. We text more than we study The Text. And our eyes aren't fixed on Jesus. They're fixed on our iPhones and iPads—emphasis on "i." Then we wonder why God feels so distant. It's because we're hugging the rim for safety.

We want joy without sacrifice.

We want character without suffering.

We want success without failure.

We want gain without pain.

We want a testimony without the test.

The character of God is a Grand Canyon. In the words of A. W. Tozer, "Eternity will not be long enough to learn all He is, or to praise Him for all He has done." But you don't get to know God by looking at Him from a distance. You have to hike into the depths of His power and the heights of His holiness. You have to go rim to rim with God.

It's not enough to sit in a church service for sixty minutes. We don't get credit for an audit. Going to church is a good thing, but sitting in a pew for sixty minutes is not God's ultimate plan for our lives. Church can undermine His plan by becoming a subtle form of spiritual codependency. We let someone else worship for us, study for us, and pray for us.

That's when church attenders become rim huggers.

Are you a hugger or a hiker?

TAKE A HIKE

This year we'll take twenty-five mission trips as a church. Our goal is fifty-two trips a year so that a mission team is coming and going all the time. Here's why we place priority on mission trips: it turns huggers into hikers! One mission trip is worth more than fifty-two sermons!

We are already educated way beyond the level of our obedience. What we need most is not another sermon. Please don't misinterpret what I'm saying. We need to study the Word of God diligently. But we don't need to know more. We need to do more with what we know. At the end of the day, God will not say, "Well thought, Intellectual," or "Well said, Orator." There is only one commendation: "Well done, good and faithful servant!"

I have a simple take on spiritual maturity. It's all about the *theoretical* becoming *experiential*. When you first read a verse of Scripture, it's nothing more than a theory because you haven't personally experienced it yet. Until you experience it for yourself, God's grace is theoretical. Once you experience it, it becomes the reality that redefines your life. The same is true of His promises. You have to prove them by putting them into practice. Then when God delivers, theory becomes reality. So over time, the Bible becomes less theoretical and more experiential. Verse by verse, the Bible becomes your spiritual reality—a reality that is far more real than the reality you can perceive with your five senses.

In the Hebrew language, there is no distinction between *knowing* and *doing*. Knowing is doing and doing is knowing. In other words, if you aren't doing it, then you don't really know it. You're a rim hugger.

Take a hike!

It's time to leave your fear at the rim.

Give God everything you've got—100 percent. Love God with *all* your heart, soul, mind, and strength. Don't just worship God with words. Worship God with blood, sweat, and tears. It's more than sincere sentiments. It's sweat equity in kingdom causes.

You cannot be the hands and feet of Jesus if you're sitting on your butt.

Church is not a spectator sport. You cannot *go to church* because *you are the church*. Church is not a building with a specific address. Church is not a gathering at a certain time. If you *are* the church, then church is happening whenever and wherever you are!

Your workplace is your mission field.

Your job is your sermon.

Your colleagues are your congregation.

That's why we often end our services with this benediction.

When you leave this place, you don't leave the presence of God. You take the presence of God with you wherever you go.

NINE

CLIMB THE CLIFF

Saul was staying on the outskirts of Gibeah under a pomegranate tree in Migron. With him were about six hundred men.

1 Samuel 14:2

On a transatlantic flight from Ethiopia to DC, I watched a film called *We Bought a Zoo*. Matt Damon plays the role of a British writer, Benjamin Mee, who rescues a failing zoo while coming to terms with his life as a widower and single father. One line from the film is unforgettable: "Sometimes all you need is twenty seconds of insane courage."

Twenty seconds of insane courage.

That's all it takes.

That's about how long it took for Peter to get out of the boat in the middle of the Sea of the Galilee. That's about how long it took for David to charge Goliath. That's about how long it took for Zacchaeus to climb the sycamore tree.

History turns on a dime, and the dime is a defining decision that takes about twenty seconds of insane courage. But if you have the courage to take that one step of faith and climb the cliff, it will change your life forever.

That's about how long it took for me to surrender my life to Jesus Christ.

That's about how long it took for me to call Lora to ask her out on our first date.

That's about how long it took to say *yes* to a church plant in Washington, DC.

Twenty seconds of insane courage.

That's all it takes.

What difficult decision do you need to make?

What tough conversation do you need to have?

What crazy risk do you need to take?

HOLY CRAZY

Can't you see Saul snacking on seeds while reclining in the shade of a pomegranate tree? I bet some of the lowest-ranking privates were even fanning him! Instead of picking a fight with the enemy, the leader of Israel's army is picking pomegranates. And it shouldn't come as a surprise—Saul had a long history of letting others fight his battles for him. Saul was a rim hugger! But his son Jonathan is anything but. Jonathan is a cliff climber.

Saul was playing not to lose. Jonathan was playing to win. And that's the difference between fear and faith. If you let fear dictate your decisions, you will live defensively, reactively, cautiously. Living by faith is playing offense with your life. And it's the difference between holding out on God and going all out for God.

Twenty seconds of insane courage.

I can't think of a better description than Jonathan picking a fight with the Philistines. It was crazy, but if God is in it, it's holy crazy.

Don't be surprised if people mock you, criticize you, and laugh at you when you do something crazy. In fact, if you aren't being criticized, it's cause for concern. People may think you're crazy when you climb a cliff, but the only other option is for them to think you're normal. Do you want to be normal? Me neither! Normal is the last thing I want to be!

I'm sure the other eleven disciples would periodically make flailing motions to Peter, mocking him for sinking in the Sea of Galilee, but *they* never walked on water, did they? Have you ever noticed how most people who criticize water walkers do so from the comfortable confines of a boat? And most people who criticize cliff climbers do so from low elevations.

David's brothers criticized him for challenging Goliath, but David made headlines while his brothers sat on the sidelines! And I'm sure the crowd got a kick out of a tax collector climbing a tree to get a glimpse of Jesus, but *they* didn't get invited to lunch with Jesus.

So what motivated Jonathan to climb the cliff? What triggered the twenty seconds of insane courage?

Let me set the scene.

During the early days of Saul's kingship, the Philistines controlled the western border of Israel and battle lines were drawn at the pass called Mikmash. Saul seemed content to sit on the sideline, but Jonathan wanted to be on the front line.

"Come, let's go over to the Philistine outpost on the other side."

One step of faith is all it takes to leave fear behind. It's often the longest, hardest, and scariest step. But when we make a move that is motivated by God's glory, it moves the heart and hand of God.

There comes a moment in our lives when enough is enough. We refuse to remain the same.

This is that moment for Jonathan.

The New Living Translation captions it "Jonathan's Daring Plan." To be perfectly honest, it seems like a dumb plan. Jonathan exposes himself to the enemy in broad daylight and concedes the high ground. Then he comes up with this sign to determine whether or not to engage the enemy.

> "But if they say, 'Come up to us,' we will climb up, because that will be our sign that the LORD has given them into our hands."

If I'm making up the signs, I do the exact opposite! If *they* come down to us, that'll be our sign. Or better yet, if they fall off the cliff, that'll be our sign. Jonathan chooses the most difficult, dangerous, and daring option that exists. But that's why I love it. When did we start believing that Jesus died to keep us safe? He died to make us dangerous! I'm not sure which was more dangerous—climbing the cliff or fighting the Philistines. There was no guarantee that Jonathan would even survive the climb. And even if he made it to the top, Jonathan and his armor-bearer were outnumbered ten to one.

Can you imagine sword fighting after climbing a cliff? But what a picture of what all out is all about! It's not looking for the easy way out. It's an all-out assault. It's not taking the path of least resistance. It's committing to the path of greatest glory, and that usually means the most difficult and dangerous option available. Jonathan knew that if he pulled off this against-all-odds upset, God would get all the glory.

So what motivated Jonathan? What triggered the twenty seconds of insane courage?

It's impossible to psychoanalyze someone who lived thousands of years ago, but one statement reveals Jonathan's MO. It's the key code in his operating system. And it's one of my favorite sentences in all of Scripture.

"Perhaps the LORD will act in our behalf."

I think most people operate out of the opposite mentality: perhaps the Lord *won't* act in our behalf. They let fear dictate their decisions instead of faith. So they end up under a pomegranate tree on the outskirts of Gibeah.

Our lack of guts is really a lack of faith. But cliff climbers would rather fall on their face than sit on their butt. They'd rather make mistakes than miss opportunities. Cliff climbers know that one step of faith can create a tipping point that changes not only *their* destiny but the course of history. And that's precisely what happened in the wake of Jonathan's bold move.

So on that day the LORD saved Israel.

But this day could be *that day*. And all it takes is one defining decision.

I recently spoke at a college commencement. Let me share the manifesto I shared with them.

Quit living as if the purpose of life is to arrive safely at death.

Set God-sized goals. Pursue God-ordained passions. Go after a dream that is destined to fail without divine intervention.

Keep asking questions. Keep making mistakes. Keep seeking God.

Stop pointing out problems and become part of the solution. Stop repeating the past and start creating the future. Stop playing it safe and start taking risks.

Expand your horizons. Accumulate experiences. Enjoy the journey.

Find every excuse you can to celebrate everything you can.

Live like today is the first day and last day of your life.

Don't let what's wrong with you keep you from worshiping what's right with God.

Burn sinful bridges. Blaze new trails.

Don't let fear dictate your decisions. Take a flying leap of faith.

Quit holding out. Quit holding back.

Go all in with God. Go all out for God.

PICK A FIGHT

I have a friend, Bob Goff, who is full of whimsy. We had dinner one night after he spoke at National Community Church, and Bob challenged us to *take over a country*! He wasn't kidding! With a grin on his face, he said, "Why not?" And why wouldn't Bob challenge us, after the way God used this one man to impact the nation of Uganda?

There are two kinds of people in the world—those who ask *why* and those who ask *why not*. *Why* people look for excuses. *Why not* people look for opportunities. *Why* people are afraid of making mistakes. *Why not* people don't want to miss out on God-ordained opportunities!

I first met Bob at the National Prayer Breakfast in Washington, DC. He was on a panel dealing with human trafficking. Through a crazy confluence of events that only God could have orchestrated, Bob was named honorary consul for the Republic of Uganda to the United States. And he's a U.S. citizen.

Much of Bob's work in Uganda involves fighting for those who can't fight for themselves. Every year, witch doctors kill hundreds of children as ritual sacrifices. A little boy named Charlie was supposed to be one of them, but despite being brutally disfigured, he managed to escape with his life. Bob prosecuted and got the very first conviction against a witch doctor in the history of the country. He also became friends with Charlie. He flew Charlie to the U.S., where he could get the surgical intervention he needed, and secured a scholarship so Charlie can get a college education when that day arrives.

It was during that panel discussion that Bob made an offhanded comment that has become a personal mantra: *pick a fight*. That single statement stirred something deep within my soul.

That's exactly what Jonathan did. He decided to pick a fight with the Philistines. He was tired of backing down, so he stood up. He was tired of playing defense, so he decided to go on the offensive. He was tired of settling for the status quo, so he decided to disrupt it.

How do we pick a fight?

It starts when we get on our knees. Prayer is picking a fight with the Enemy. It's spiritual warfare. Intercession transports us from the sidelines to the front lines without going anywhere. Prayer is the difference between us fighting for God and God fighting for us. But we can't just hit our knees. We also have to take a step, take a stand. And when we do, we never know what God will do next.

Here's the rest of the story.

After getting the conviction against the witch doctor, Bob visited him in prison. That witch doctor gave his life to Jesus Christ and is now preaching the gospel to other prisoners. It's not about winning a battle. It's about winning people over!

PLAY OFFENSE

The cosmic battle between good and evil rages all around us all the time, yet we live like its peacetime. Two thousand years ago, Jesus rallied the troops and sounded the charge with a call to spiritual arms.

"I will build my church, and the gates of Hades will not overcome it."

Gates are defensive measures. Faithfulness is not holding the fort. It's storming the gates of hell and taking back enemy territory that belongs to God.

I'm afraid we've reduced righteousness to the absence of wrongness, but goodness is not the absence of badness. You can do nothing wrong and still do nothing right. Remember the parable of the bags of gold?

We don't sit still for very long at National Community Church. We're always thinking about what's next. We have a little motto that has become part of our mind-set: *Go. Set. Ready.* That may seem backward, but it's the way we keep moving forward. If we wait till we're ready, we'll be waiting the rest of our lives. We'll never have the human resources or financial resources to do what God has called us to do. And if we do, our dream is too small.

FACE YOUR FEARS

A few months ago, I had coffee with a Washington, DC, Council member. I wanted to get his pulse on the greatest needs in our city to see how we as the church could help meet them. We had a great conversation that ranged from fatherlessness to homelessness.

At the end of our conversation, I asked this Council member if I could pray for him. He had just decided to throw his hat into the DC mayoral race, so I knew he was feeling the pressure of politics at an all-new level. When he didn't give me an answer right away, I wondered if I had offended him. He looked me in the eye and said, "Pray that I don't let fear dictate my decisions."

If the election had been held right then, he would have gotten my vote.

In the town where I live, decisions are often made on the

basis of opinion polls instead of moral principles. But all of us are subject to pride, lust, anger, and jealousy. Those dictators often affect our decisions in subconscious ways. But the worst dictator is fear. It governs through intimidation. And the largest Philistine among them is the fear of failure.

You have to choose a dictator. You can let fear dictate your decisions, or you can let faith dictate your decisions.

BETTER SAFE THAN SORRY

It's important to make a distinction between *personality* issues and *spiritual* issues. Some people seem to be wired for risk, while others aren't. All of us land at different places on the risk spectrum, but just because you aren't a natural risk taker doesn't mean you get an exemption because of personality.

Think of it this way. There are spiritual gifts like mercy, faith, or generosity that enable people to *set the standard*, so to speak. But just because you don't have that spiritual gift doesn't mean you aren't held to any standard at all. Even if you aren't gifted in that way, you're still called to live mercifully, faithfully, and generously. You might not *set the standard*, but you need to *meet the standard*. There is a baseline that all of us are called to. When the opportunity presents itself, we need to show mercy, exercise faith, and give generously. In the same sense, all of us are called to take risks. If it doesn't involve risk, it doesn't exercise faith.

A pair of psychologists from the University of Michigan conducted a fascinating study a decade ago that reframed the way I think about fear. Volunteers wore an electrode cap that enabled researchers to analyze brain activity in response to winning and losing during a computer-simulated betting game. With each bet, the medial frontal cortex showed increased electrical activity within a matter of milliseconds. But what intrigued the researchers was that medial frontal negativity showed a larger dip after a loss than the rise in medial frontal positivity after a win. Researchers came to a simple yet profound conclusion: *losses loom larger than gains*.

So many people play not to lose. It's our neurological default setting. We fixate on sins of commission instead of sins of omission. And maybe that is why we approach the will of God with a "better safe than sorry" mentality.

Most of us are far too tentative when it comes to the will of God. We're so afraid of making the wrong decision that we make no decision. And no decision is a decision. It's called indecision.

TAKE A STAND

On October 31, 1517, a monk named Martin Luther picked a fight with the religious establishment. He had the audacity to challenge the status quo by attacking the selling of indulgences. Luther posted ninety-five theses on the doors of All Saints' Church in Wittenberg, Germany, and ignited the Protestant Reformation.

I had the privilege of visiting Wittenberg a few years ago on Reformation Day. What's amazing to me is the way a little-known monk in a tiny hamlet in the middle of nowhere could impact history the way he did. But that's what happens when you have no fear.

I don't think Martin Luther knew he was making history

as he made history, but our small acts of courage have a domino effect. When we do what's right, regardless of circumstances or consequences, we set the table for God to turn the tables. All we need to do is stand up, step in, or step out.

At the Diet of Worms in 1521, Martin Luther was summoned by the Holy Roman emperor Charles V and put on trial for his beliefs. Martin Luther mustered the moral courage to take a stand: "My conscience is taken captive by God's word, I cannot and will not recant anything. For to act against our conscience is neither safe for us, nor open to us. On this I take my stand. I can do no other. God help me. Amen."

Whom do you need to stand up for?

The homeless? The fatherless? The voiceless?

Forget safe! Climb the cliff. Pick the fight.

TEN

BUILD THE ARK

By faith Noah, when warned about things not yet seen, in holy fear built an ark to save his family.
HEBREWS 11:7

In 1948, Korczak Ziolkowski was commissioned by Lakota Chief Henry Standing Bear to design a mountain carving that would honor the famous war leader Crazy Horse. The great irony is that Crazy Horse didn't even allow himself to be photographed. You have to wonder how he'd feel about a 563-foot-high statue of himself carved in the granite face of the Black Hills. Since Korczak's death in 1982, the Ziolkowski family has carried on their father's vision and continued carving. Their projected date of completion is 2050, just shy of the one-hundred-year mark.

One hundred years devoted to one task!

But Crazy Horse falls twenty years short of how long it took Noah to build the ark. It took Noah 120 years to build the ark. If they had named boats back then like they do now, I think *Holy Crazy* would have been spot-on. Noah's ark project ranks as one of history's largest and longest construction projects. I think we fail to appreciate it for what it is—a really big boat built a really long time ago! Just pause and appreciate.

The ark measured 300 cubits in length, 50 cubits in width, and 30 cubits in height. In the Hebrew system of measurement, a cubit was the equivalent of 17.5 inches. That means the ark was the length of one and a half football fields. Not until the late nineteenth century did a ship that size get constructed again, yet the 30:5:3 design ratio is still considered the golden mean for stability during storms at sea. The internal volume of the ark was 1,518,750 cubit feet—the equivalent of 569 boxcars. If the average animal was the size of a sheep, it had capacity for 125,000 animals. To put that into perspective, there are 2,000 animals from 400 different species at the National Zoo in Washington, DC. That means you could fit 60 National Zoos on board Noah's ark!

Building the ark required a rare combination of brains and brawn. It took Mensa amounts of creative genius. After all, it was the first boat ever built. It's not like it came with an instruction manual. It was also backbreaking work. It took buckets of blood, sweat, and tears. But even more than brains and brawn, it took an incalculable amount of faith to build the ark.

Who builds a boat in the desert? Who hammers away for 120 years at something they might not even need? According to Jewish tradition, Noah didn't just start building the ark. He planted trees first. After they were fully grown, he cut down the trees, sawed them into planks, and built the boat.

It's not a sprint. It's a marathon.

Don't worry about public opinion.

Live for the applause of nail-scarred hands.

LONG OBEDIENCE

When people asked Korczak Ziolkowski how he could devote his entire life to one task, he simply said, "When your life is over, the world will ask you only one question: 'Did you do what you were supposed to do?'"

That's not just a good question. That's *the* question.

Did you do what you were supposed to do?

Noah built the ark because God commanded it. It's what he was supposed to do. And when everything was said and done, it was the longest act of obedience recorded in Scripture. From start to finish, Noah's one act of obedience took 43,800 days!

I'm supposed to write books.

I actually scored below average on an aptitude exam for writing when I was in graduate school, but I knew I was called to write. I also knew my lack of aptitude would require greater reliance on God's anointing. That's how God gets more glory!

For thirteen years, I was a frustrated writer. I couldn't complete a single manuscript. I grew to despise my birthday because it felt like an annual reminder of an unfulfilled dream. When I finally published my first book, *In a Pit with a Lion on a Snowy Day*, I felt more relief than joy. I knew I had finally done exactly what I was supposed to do.

Writing is more than combining the twenty-six letters of the English alphabet into words and sentences and paragraphs and chapters. For me, writing a book is an act of obedience that usually takes four to six months of early mornings and late nights.

I don't write with a keyboard.

I pray with it.

I worship with it.

I dream with it.

Setting my alarm for early in the morning and sitting down at my keyboard are acts of obedience. It's what I'm supposed to do. The harder it is and the longer it takes, the more God is glorified.

No matter what tool you use in your trade—a hammer, a keyboard, a mop, a football, a spreadsheet, a microphone, or an espresso machine—using it is an act of obedience. It's the mechanism whereby you worship God. It's the way you do what you are supposed to do.

THE POINT OF PRECEDENCE

I don't know what went through Noah's mind when God told him to build a boat, but I'm guessing it was either *You've got to be kidding* or *You've got to be crazy!* Noah didn't even have a cognitive category for what God was calling him to build. It was absolutely unprecedented. Yet he obeyed every jot and tittle of revelation God gave him.

Noah did everything just as God commanded him.

I want God to reveal the second step before I take the first step of faith. But if I don't take the first step, God generally won't reveal the next step. We've got to be obedient to the measure of revelation God has given us if we want more of it. We want more revelation before we obey more, but God wants more obedience before He reveals more.

Most of us will only follow Christ to the point of precedence. But no further. We're afraid of doing what we've never done because it's unfamiliar territory. So we leave unclaimed the new gifts, new anointings, and new dreams that God wants to give to us.

If you want God to do something new, you cannot keep doing what you've always done. You've got to push past the fear of the unknown. We want a money-back guarantee before we take a step of obedience, but that eliminates faith from the equation. Sometimes we need to take a flying leap of faith.

We need to step into the conflict without knowing if we can resolve it. We need to share our faith without knowing how our friends will react to it. We need to pray for a miracle without knowing how God will answer. We need to put ourselves in a situation that activates a spiritual gift we've never exercised before. And we need to go after a dream that is destined to fail without divine intervention.

If we want to discover new lands, we've got to lose sight of the shore. We've got to leave the Land of Familiarity behind. We've got to sail past the predictable. And when we do, we develop a spiritual hunger for the unprecedented and lose our appetite for the habitual. We also get a taste of God's favor.

FOUND FAVOR

Noah found favor in the eyes of the Lord.

The favor of God is what God can do for you that you cannot do for yourself.

It's His favor that opens the door of opportunity.

It's His favor that turns opposition into support.

It's His favor that can help you land the promotion, make the list, or seal the deal.

I pray for the favor of God more than anything else. I pray it for my books. I pray it for National Community Church. And I pray it for my children. I've prayed it—based on Luke 2:52—for my children thousands of times:

May you grow in wisdom and stature, and in favor with God and man.

So how do you find favor? The short answer is obedience!

It starts by surrendering our lives to the lordship of Jesus Christ. Jesus proclaimed the favor of God in His very first sermon. Then He sealed the deal with His death and resurrection. Favor is a function of surrender. If we don't hold out on God, God will not hold out on us.

No good thing does God withhold from those who walk uprightly.

We position ourselves for the favor of God by walking in humility and purity. Every promise is *yes* in Christ. Every spiritual blessing becomes our birthright. And if we consecrate ourselves to Him, His favor will be our vanguard and rear guard.

In one respect, all we need is the favor found at the foot of the cross. But the favor of God is not limited to the spiritual realm. His favor extends into the material realm as well. In Noah's life, it translated into ingenious inventions. He was the Leonardo da Vinci and Thomas Edison of his era. Noah didn't just build the first boat and pioneer the shipbuilding industry. According to Jewish tradition, Noah invented the plow, the scythe, the hoe, and a number of other implements used for cultivating the ground. The favor of God translated into God-ideas.

It doesn't matter what you do, God wants to help you do it. He wants to favor your business plan, your political campaign, your manuscript, your lesson plan, your legal brief, your film, and your sales pitch. But you've got to position yourself for that favor by acting in obedience. And if God knows He'll get the glory, He will bless you beyond your ability, beyond your resources, and beyond your fears.

IF YOU BUILD IT

One of my all-time favorite movie lines is from the 1989 film *Field of Dreams.* Kevin Costner plays the role of novice-farmer-and-baseball-lover Ray Kinsella. While walking through a corn field, Ray hears a faint whisper: "If you build it, they will come." Ray literally bets the farm and builds a baseball diamond in the middle of nowhere. And after much soul-searching and penny-pinching, the ghosts of baseball past mysteriously appear and play ball.

More than a decade ago, I had a "field of dreams" moment. In my case, it wasn't a corn field in Iowa. It was a crack house on Capitol Hill. One day as I walked by a dilapidated nuisance property that I had passed hundreds of times before, I heard the still small voice of the Holy Spirit: *This crack house would make a great coffeehouse.* It's not easy to discern between a good idea and a God-idea, but I was pretty certain I was hearing the Holy Spirit.

The original asking price for that postage-stamp piece of property was $1 million because of its location. We couldn't afford to buy it, so we circled our Promised Land in prayer for five years! The more we prayed, the more the price went down.

And despite the fact that four people offered more money for it than we did, we eventually purchased it for $325,000.

The original vision was to create a place where church and community could cross paths. And while it seemed a little crazy for a church to build a coffeehouse, the method to our madness was modeled by Jesus Himself. Jesus didn't just hang out with religious people at religious places. He hung out at wells—natural gathering places in ancient culture. That's when it dawned on us that coffeehouses are postmodern wells! But instead of water, we serve coffee. Actually, coffee with a cause. Ebenezers Coffeehouse gives every penny of profit to missions. Since our inception, more than a million customers have walked through our doors, and we've given away more than $750,000 to kingdom causes. We've also been voted the #1 coffeehouse in the metro DC area.

Churches are supposed to build church buildings, not coffeehouses. I understand that. And when God originally gave us the vision, it was unprecedented. Which is a nice way of saying it was unsafe. But kingdom causes often start out as crazy ideas! And if God is in it, it's holy crazy. No one on our staff had any entrepreneurial experience whatsoever. None of us had even worked in a coffeehouse. And I didn't even drink coffee! But that isn't the issue. The only issue is this:

Is this what we were supposed to do?

AS IF

Faith is the willingness to look foolish.

Noah looked foolish building an ark in the desert. Sarah looked foolish buying maternity clothes at ninety.

Moses looked foolish asking Pharaoh to let his slaves go. The Israelite army looked foolish marching around Jericho blowing trumpets. David looked foolish attacking Goliath with a slingshot. The Wise Men looked foolish following a star to Timbuktu. Peter looked foolish stepping out of the boat in the middle of the lake in the middle of the night. And Jesus looked foolhardy hanging half naked on the cross.

But the results speak for themselves, don't they?

Noah stayed afloat during the flood. Sarah gave birth to Isaac. Moses delivered Israel out of Egypt. The walls of Jericho came tumbling down. David defeated Goliath. The Wise Men found the Messiah. Peter walked on water. And Jesus rose from the dead.

If you aren't willing to look foolish, you're foolish. And that's why so many people have never built an ark, killed a giant, or walked on water.

There comes a moment when we quit hedging our bets. We quit playing it safe. We quit doing what we've always done. We need to build the ark, or at least plant some trees or saw some planks!

Faith is acting as if God has already answered. And acting as if God has answered means acting on our prayers, even if it takes 120 years.

KEEP HAMMERING AWAY

I think it's safe to say that Noah didn't get much sleep on the ark. He was feeding, cleaning, and caring for thousands of animals around the clock. And it must have smelled to high heaven. Did you know that African elephants produce eighty pounds of waste per day? It was smelly and messy. Obedience is hard work, and it gets harder.

The blessings of God will complicate your life, but unlike sin, they will complicate your life in the way it should be complicated. Marrying Lora complicated my life. Praise God. We have three complications named Parker, Summer, and Josiah. I can't imagine my life without those complications. And National Community Church is far more complicated now than it was when we had only nineteen people!

No matter what vision God has given you, I can predict it will *take longer* and *be harder* than you ever imagined. If a decade sounds like a long time to patiently pursue a God-ordained passion, try twelve decades! It's amazing what God can do if you keep hammering away for 120 years!

I admire plotters—people who can see into the future and cast a vision.

I admire plodders even more—people who put one foot in front of the other, one day at a time!

Going all out for God is not just about getting where God wants you to go. It's about who you become in the process. And it's not about how quickly you get there. It's about how far you go.

Going all out is going the distance.

It's crossing the finish line the way the apostle did:

I have fought the good fight, I have finished the race, and I have remained faithful.

ELEVEN

GRAB YOUR OXGOAD

After Ehud came Shamgar son of Anath, who struck down six hundred Philistines with an oxgoad. He too saved Israel.

JUDGES 3:31

One sentence.

After Ehud came Shamgar son of Anath, who struck down six hundred Philistines with an oxgoad.

That is all the press Shamgar gets in Scripture, but this one byline tells me everything I need to know about him. One daring decision and one farm implement result in deliverance for the entire nation of Israel.

Israel was in a state of spiritual anarchy and political tyranny. But one man refused to be ruled by unrighteousness. He decided to disrupt the status quo, and he did it with an oxgoad.

Next to David, Shamgar has to rank as one of history's most improbable heroes. And just like the shepherd-turned-king, this farmer-turned-warrior transformed a tool of his trade into a weapon of war.

Shamgar had no army, no alliance, and no artillery. All he had was an oxgoad—a long stick used by a farmer to prod his animals. But he did not let what he could not do keep him from doing what he could. After all, God plus one equals a majority. And if God is for you, who can be against you? So Shamgar grabbed his oxgoad and charged the enemy armies. He looked as foolhardy as David charging Goliath with a slingshot. The enemy chuckled at his makeshift weaponry until he started wielding it. Then the look in his eyes struck fear in their hearts.

Courage doesn't wait until situational factors turn in one's favor. It doesn't wait until a plan is perfectly formed. It doesn't wait until the tide of popular opinion is turned. Courage only waits for one thing: a green light from God.

A LITTLE CRAZY

Like Shamgar, Cori Wittman grew up on a farm. After college, Cori moved to Washington, DC, and started working on Capitol Hill. She got involved at National Community Church, and she went on our first mission trip to Thailand to work with The Well, a ministry that rescues women out of the sex industry. During that trip, Cori prayed a dangerous prayer: *Lord, break my heart for the things that break Your heart.* One conversation with a Thai farm girl who ended up in Bangkok's red-light district because of circumstances beyond her control did just that. She decided to quit her job and move to Thailand as a full-time missionary. She started out working during the night shift in the red-light district of Bangkok, ministering to women trapped in the web of the sex trade. She is now trying to stop the problem before it starts by piloting a program for teens in rural Thailand. This single twentysomething is mentoring and mothering seven teen girls.

Thailand is a nonconfrontational culture, which makes change very challenging. But Cori is gracefully challenging the status quo. She is fighting governmental corruption, sex solicitation, and illiteracy with her oxgoad. That's what going all out for Christ is all about. It's attacking problems with whatever oxgoad God has given you. It's more than just having a heart for Christ. It's being His hands and His feet.

HERE AM I

In God's kingdom, calling trumps credentials every time! God doesn't call the qualified. He qualifies the called. And the litmus test isn't experience or expertise. It's availability and teachability. If you are willing to go when God gives you a green light, He will take you to inaccessible places to do impossible things.

> *Then I heard the voice of the Lord saying, "Whom shall I send? And who will go for us?"*
> *And I said, "Here am I. Send me!"*

Abraham. Jacob. Joseph. Moses. Samuel. David. Isaiah.
They all have one thing in common.
They all said, "Here am I."
It's God's job to get us where He wants us to go. Our job is to make ourselves available anytime, anyplace. Like a

doctor on call or a police officer on duty or a firefighter on shift, it's our readiness to respond that God is looking for. Sometimes it's a simple prompting to go out of our way to love our next-door neighbor. Sometimes it's a calling to move halfway around the world. But it always starts with the little three-word prayer of availability: *Here am I.*

That's what Samuel said when he heard the still small voice of the Holy Spirit.

That's what Moses said at the burning bush.

That's what Caleb said when he finally stepped foot into the Promised Land.

That's what Isaiah said when King Uzziah died.

Are you willing to do something a little crazy?

Shamgar may have been the least qualified person to deliver Israel. For starters, he likely wasn't even an Israelite. His name is Hurrian in origin. He could have rationalized inaction in a dozen different ways. *I don't have the right weapon. I can't do this by myself. These aren't even my people.* If we look for an excuse, we will always find one. If we don't, we won't. When it comes to making excuses, we are infinitely creative. What if we channeled that creativity into finding solutions instead of finding excuses?

When God stirs our spirit or breaks our heart, we cannot sit back. We've got to step up and step in. We've got to go all in by going all out. If we have the courage to make the choice or take the risk, it will become the defining moment of our lives.

REDEFINING SUCCESS

You never know what relationship, skill, experience, or attribute God will use to bring about His eternal purposes! He used a beauty pageant to strategically position Esther as queen of Persia and stop the genocide of the Jews. He used Nehemiah's diligence as a cupbearer to position him for a royal favor that would parlay into rebuilding the wall of Jerusalem. He used David's musical chops to open the palace door and give him access to the king of Israel. He used Joseph's imprisonment and his ability to interpret dreams to save two nations from famine. And he used the zeal of a mass murderer named Saul to spread the gospel via three missionary journeys while writing half of the New Testament in the process.

Do the best you can with what you have where you are.

It doesn't matter whether you're a journalist, teacher, entrepreneur, artist, politician, or lawyer. What matters is that you are using your oxgoad for God's purposes. Don't just make a living. Make a life! Make a mark! Make a difference!

ENOUGH IS ENOUGH

I think Shagmar made a decision that if he was going to go down, he was going to go down fighting. And that's the key to deliverance, whether it's from the Philistines or pride or prejudice or pornography.

You've got to go on the offensive.

You've got to pick a fight.

You've got to plan a D-day invasion.

There comes a point when *enough is enough*. We know we cannot continue down the path we are on because it's a dead end relationally, physically, or spiritually. It may not kill us, but it will eat us alive. We know we cannot keep doing what we've always done.

The good news is this: you are only one decision away from a totally different life. One risk can revolutionize your life. One change can change everything. If you start small and stay consistent, anything is possible. A 1 percent change, given enough time, can make a 99 percent difference in your life. You've got to grab your oxgoad and go for it.

Cut up your credit card.

Register for the marathon.

Apply for the graduate program.

Take the mission trip.

Set up the counseling appointment.

Stop being safe.

THE PLAINS OF HESITATION

Using the pseudonym William A. Lawrence, George W. Cecil said, "On the Plains of Hesitation bleach the bones of countless millions who, at the Dawn of Victory, sat down to wait, and waiting—died!"

I'm both a procrastinator and a perfectionist. Plus, I'm a possibility thinker. That combination of personality traits means I've had to discipline myself to make decisions and set deadlines. I've come to terms with the fact that indecision *is* a decision. Dreams without deadlines are dead in the water. Deadlines are really lifelines to achieving our goals.

When it comes to going after our goals, the greatest adversary is inertia. Unless we commit to a new course of action, we'll maintain our current rhythms and routines. It's also known as the *status quo bias*.

Good intentions aren't good enough. You need to make

the call or make the move. You need to set the deadline or set the appointment. If you don't, your bones will probably bleach on the Plains of Hesitation.

If Shamgar had focused on the fact that he was going to go up against six hundred Philistines, I bet he would have given up before he even got started. The Enemy often tries to discourage us by overwhelming us. We need to counterpunch by breaking down our goals into smaller steps. I don't know if you can overcome alcoholism or anorexia for the rest of your life, but I believe you can win the battle *today*.

Don't worry about next week or next year. Live in day-tight compartments. Can you resist temptation for twenty-four hours? Can you win the battle for one day? I know you can. So do you. And so does the Enemy.

Take it one day at a time!

ONE STEP AT A TIME

A few years ago, I climbed Half Dome at Yosemite National Park. I remember looking up at the summit and thinking, *How am I going to make it to the top?* The answer was really quite simple: *one step at a time.*

The hardest part of the hike wasn't physical. It was mental. The last leg was a sixty-degree slope to the summit that looked like a ninety-degree climb to someone who is afraid of heights. I'm afraid of heights. When I finally got to the top of Half Dome, I sat down on a large rock and noticed that someone had etched something into the rock: *If you can do this, you can do anything.*

Something inside of me clicked because I knew it was

true. I decided to attempt something I hadn't been able to do in five years of trying. I was packing 225 pounds, which isn't terribly overweight on my six foot three inch frame, but I knew I'd feel better and live longer if I could tip the scales at sub-200. I made a defining decision to do it, and then I made a daily decision to exercise more and eat less. In two months I dropped twenty-five pounds. I also dropped my cholesterol by fifty points. And I felt five years younger.

We spend far too much energy focusing on the very thing we cannot control—the outcome. What if I fall back into my bad habit? What if my romantic efforts aren't reciprocated? What if I don't hit my target weight or get my dream job?

Don't worry about results. Focus on doing the right thing for the right reason. And don't buy into the lie that it can't be done! It will take all-out effort, but you can do all things through Christ, who gives you strength.

A failed attempt is not failing.

Failing is not trying.

If you are trying, you are succeeding.

That's what going all out is all about.

It's giving it everything you've got.

It's not safe.

PART FOUR

NOT MY OWN

TWELVE

SDG

Johann Sebastian Bach was to classical music what William Shakespeare was to English literature and Sir Isaac Newton was to physics. His body of work includes 256 cantatas. My personal favorite is *Jesu, Joy of Man's Desiring*. Nearly four centuries after its original writing, it's still one of the most popular soundtracks to one of life's most momentous occasions—the bridal entrance at a wedding ceremony.

The reason *Toccata and Fugue in D Minor* or *Mass in B Minor* touch the soul is that they come from the soul. Bach's cantatas didn't originate as music. They were prayers before they were songs. Before Bach started scoring a sheet of music, he would scrawl *J.J.—Jesu, juva*—at the very top. It was the simplest of prayers: *Jesus, help me.*

Then, at the completion of every composition, Bach inscribed three letters in the margin of his music: SDG. Those three letters stood for the Latin phrase, *Soli Deo Gloria—to the glory of God alone. Soli Deo Gloria* was one of the rallying cries of the Protestant Reformation, but Bach personalized it. His life was a unique translation of that singular motive. So is yours. No one can glorify God *like you* or *for you*. Your life is an original score.

Imagine if filmmakers and politicians and entrepreneurs followed suit. What kind of cultural impact would we have if our scripts and bills and business plans originated as prayers? Imagine students scribbling SDG on their essays for AP American History, mechanics etching SDG on mufflers and motors, or doctors scrawling SDG on their prescriptions.

It's not about *what* you do.

It's about *why* you do what you do.

Ultimately, it's about *who* you do it for.

In God's kingdom, it's our motivations that matter most. If you do the right thing for the wrong reason, it doesn't even count. God judges the motives of the heart, and He only rewards those who do the right thing for the right reason.

SDG is living for an audience of one. It's doing the right thing for the right reason. It's living for the applause of nail-scarred hands.

Just Jesus.

Nothing more, nothing less, nothing else.

THE CHIEF END OF MAN

The very first tenet of the Westminster Shorter Catechism is worth memorizing. It's the least common denominator when it comes to living a purpose-driven life.

Man's chief end is to glorify God, and to enjoy Him forever.

We exist for one reason and one reason alone: *to glorify God, and to enjoy Him forever.* It's not about you at all. It's all about Him.

Soli Deo Gloria is the Rosetta Stone that makes life make sense. It's not about success and failure. It's not about good days and bad days. It's not about wealth or poverty. It's not about health or sickness. It's not even about life or death. It's about glorifying God in whatever circumstance you find yourself in.

Anyway. Anywhere. Anyhow.

Whenever. Wherever. Whatever.

There is no circumstance in which you cannot glorify God.

WHATEVER

The word *whatever* isn't my favorite word as a parent, but I think it's redeemable. It's one of my one-word prayers to God. When used in a submissive way, the word *whatever* is a statement of absolute surrender.

Think of Gethsemane, the garden where Jesus Himself wrestled with the will of God. He said to His Father, "Take this cup from Me." It was a reference to the cup of wrath. Jesus knew He'd have to drink it to the dregs, but before He did, He asked the Father if He would take it away, if there was any other way. But then He qualified his request with the ultimate all-in prayer: "Not My will, but Yours be done."

This was His *whatever* prayer.

There are two *whatever* verses in Scripture. Both start with the same all-inclusive phrase: *whatever you do.*

Whatever you do, work at it with all your heart, as working for the Lord, not for human masters.

Ultimately, I hope you love what you do and do what you

love. Find a job that you would want to do even if you didn't
get paid to do it. That isn't the reality at every stage of life.
Sometimes you need to have a job you don't like, but you can
still glorify God by doing a good job at a bad job. And at least
you have a job!

Anybody can do a good job at a good job, but there is
something God-glorifying about doing a good job at a bad
job. Anybody can be nice to a nice boss, but there is something
God-glorifying when you love like Jesus in a godless work
environment.

MUNDANE MIRACLES

Now here's the other *whatever* verse.

> *So whether you eat or drink or whatever you do, do it*
> *all for the glory of God.*

How do you eat and drink for the glory of God?

Paul is using the daily rituals of eating and drinking
to make an all-encompassing point: *even the most mundane*
of activities is absolutely miraculous. You take approximately
23,000 breaths every day, but when was the last time you
thanked God for one of them? We tend to thank God for the
things that take our breath away. And that's fine. But maybe
we should thank Him for every other breath too!

SDG is the *why* behind every *what*. It's the *why* behind
every *whatever*. Our prayers tend to focus on external circumstances more than internal attitudes because we'd rather have
God change our circumstances than change us. It's a lot easier

that way. But we miss the point altogether. It's the worst of circumstances that often brings out the best in us.

You can be saved without suffering, but you cannot be sanctified without suffering. That doesn't mean you seek it out, but it does mean you see it for what it is. It's an opportunity to glorify God.

GIVE AND TAKE AWAY

No one in the history of humankind has endured more loss in less time than Job. He lost everything—his family, his health, and his wealth—in a matter of moments. He endured unbelievable heartache, unimaginable loss. But when his world falls apart, Job falls to the ground in worship.

> *Naked I came from my mother's womb,*
> *and naked I will depart.*
> *The LORD gave and the LORD has taken away;*
> *may the name of the LORD be praised.*

Our friends Jason and Shelly Yost started a wonderful organization called New Rhythm that advocates for adoption. After going through the legal process themselves, they adopted a precious little girl they named Mariah. But a few days after taking her into their home, she was taken out of their hands by the birth mother.

I saw Jason and Shelly a few days later at a retreat where I was speaking and Jason was leading worship. I was floored by the first song he sang: "Blessed Be Your Name." The lyrics are inspired by the story of Job. In fact, the chorus restates this very verse: *You give and take away.* I have certain verses that I call *fallback positions.* When all else fails, I fall back on the things I know to be true. This is one of those verses. It's His prerogative to give. And it's His prerogative to take away. But there is one thing that can never be taken from you, and that is Jesus Christ. And if you have Jesus, then you have everything you will ever need for all of eternity.

Everything – Jesus = Nothing

Jesus + Nothing = Everything

It's not safe, but it is simple.

THIRTEEN

THROW DOWN
YOUR STAFF

Then the LORD asked him, "What is that in your hand?"

"A shepherd's staff," Moses replied.

"Throw it down on the ground," the LORD told him. So Moses threw down the staff, and it turned into a snake!

EXODUS 4:2–3 NLT

Nearly a hundred years ago, the Philadelphia Church in Stockholm, Sweden, sent two missionary couples to the Congo. David and Svea Flood, along with Joel and Bertha Erickson, macheted their way through the jungle to establish a mission station. During their first year, they didn't see a single convert. That didn't keep Svea from sharing the love of Jesus with a five-year-old boy who delivered fresh eggs to their back door every day.

Svea became pregnant not long after arriving, but she was

bedridden during much of the pregnancy battling malaria. She gave birth to a baby girl, Aina, on April 13, 1923, but Svea died seventeen days later. David made a casket and buried his twenty-seven-year-old wife on the mountainside overlooking the village. Grief, then bitterness, flooded his heart. David gave his daughter, Aina, to the Ericksons and returned to Sweden. He would spend the next five decades of his life trying to drown his sorrow with drink. He forewarned those he knew never to mention God's name in his presence.

The Ericksons raised Aina until she was a toddler, but both of them died within three days of each other when the villagers poisoned them. Aina was given to an American missionary couple, Arthur and Anna Berg. The Bergs renamed their adopted daughter Agnes, and called her Aggie. They eventually returned to America to pastor a church in South Dakota.

After high school, Aggie enrolled at North Central Bible College in Minneapolis, Minnesota. She met and married a fellow student, Dewey Hurst. They started a family of their own and served a number of churches as pastors. Then Dr. Hurst became president of Northwest Bible College. On their twenty-fifth wedding anniversary, the college gave the Hursts a special gift—a trip to Sweden. Aggie's sole purpose in going was to find her biological father. They searched Stockholm for five days without a trace. On the last day before departure, they got a tip that led to the third floor of a ramshackle apartment building. There they found Aggie's dad, who was on his deathbed with a failing liver.

The last words David Flood ever expected to hear were, "Papa, it's Aina." And the first words out of his mouth were filled with remorse: "I never meant to give you away." When they embraced, a fifty-year curse of bitterness was broken.

Now here's the rest of the story.

Five years later, Dewey and Aggie Hurst attended the World Pentecostal Conference in London, England. One of the speakers on opening night was Ruhigita Ndagora, the superintendent of the Pentecostal Church in Zaire. What caught Aggie's attention was the fact that Ruhigita was from the region where her parents had been missionaries half a century before. After the message, Aggie spoke to him through an interpreter. She asked if he knew of the village where she was born, and Ruhigita told her he had grown up in that village. She asked if he knew of missionaries by the name of Flood. He said, "Every day I would go to Svea Flood's back door with a basket of eggs, and she would tell me about Jesus. I don't know if she had a single convert in all of Africa besides me." Then he added, "Shortly after I accepted Christ, Svea died and her husband left. She had a baby girl named Aina, and I've always wondered what happened to her."

When Aggie revealed that she was Aina, Ruhigita Ndagora started to sob. They embraced like siblings separated since birth. Then Ruhigita said, "Just a few months ago, I placed flowers on your mother's grave. On behalf of the hundreds of churches and hundreds of thousands of believers in Zaire, thank you for letting your mother die so that so many of us could live."

Sometimes going all in feels like it's all for naught.

That's how it felt on the Saturday between Good Friday and Resurrection Sunday. The greatest spiritual victory was won on the heels of its seemingly greatest defeat. All was lost, but not for long. Three days after his crucifixion, Jesus walked out of His tomb under His own power.

In God's kingdom, failure is never final. Not if you believe in the resurrection! You won't win every spiritual battle, but the war has already been decisively won. The victory was sealed two thousand years ago when Jesus broke the seal on His tomb. It was the deathblow to death itself. And we are more than conquerors because of what Christ accomplished.

If you go all in and all out for the cause of Christ, there will be setbacks along the way. But remember this: without a crucifixion there can be no resurrection! And when you have a setback, you do not take a step back, because God is already preparing your comeback.

You never know which seed it will be. But if you plant and water, Scripture guarantees that God Himself will give the increase!

Never underestimate the ripple effect of one act of obedience.

It will never be all for nothing.

THE PATRON SAINT OF SECOND CHANCES

For forty years, Moses felt like he had failed to accomplish his God-ordained dream of delivering the Israelites out of slavery. The prince of Egypt had all the potential in the world at forty, but he felt like a lost cause at eighty. He lost everything when he lost his temper. He was both a felon and a fugitive. Instead of doing God's will God's way, he took matters into his own hands and killed an Egyptian taskmaster. And by trying to expedite God's will, he delayed it for four decades!

At some point in our lives, most of us feel like life has passed us by. That crisis presents us with a choice: throw in the towel once and for all or throw our hat back in the ring.

Too many people give up on their dreams because they feel like God has given up on them. They call it quits because they feel like it's too little, too late. But the ageless wonder serves as a timeless reminder that it's never too late to be who you might have been. Moses is the patron saint of second chances. And third. And tenth. And hundredth.

Moses was put out to pasture for forty years. But what seemed like a life sentence to Moses was really parole with a purpose. God had already put Moses through forty years of *Palace 101*. Now Moses had to pass *Wilderness 101*.

The irony of the Exodus story is that Moses thought he was unqualified, but God was leveraging every past experience to providentially prepare him for his date with destiny. No one knew the protocol of the palace like the prince of Egypt. After all, he grew up in it. And after tending sheep for forty years, he knew the ways of the wilderness—the wildlife, the watering holes, the weather patterns.

Can you think of a better way to prepare Moses to lead the sheep of Israel through the wilderness for forty years?

Going all in all for God isn't something you do once. You'll probably have a few failures before you get it right. But someday you'll celebrate the failure as much as success. Success without any failure is like a plant without any roots or a building without any foundation. Failure is the substructure that supports the superstructure of success.

National Community Church has been blessed beyond my wildest dreams. But the thing that keeps everything in perspective is our failed church plant in Chicago that predates our move to DC. I wouldn't want to go through it again, but I wouldn't trade it for anything in the world. That failure laid a foundation of humble dependence on God. Before God grew the church, He needed to grow me. But through it all, God was leading us in triumphal procession. Without a failed church plant in Chicago, we would never have landed in the nation's capital. And the crucifixion of our dream ultimately led to its resurrection.

TRIUMPHAL PROCESSION

The apostle Paul writes these words in his letter to the Corinthians:

But thanks be to God, who always leads us as captives in Christ's triumphal procession and uses us to spread the aroma of the knowledge of him everywhere.

The promise in 2 Corinthians 2:14 is an allusion to a Roman tradition. After winning a great victory, the Roman army marched through the streets of Rome with captives in their train. The triumphal procession started at the Campus Martius and led through the Circus Maximus and around Palatine Hill. Immediately after the Arch of Constantine, the procession marched along the Via Sacra to the Forum Romanum and on to Capitoline Hill.

Our triumphal procession begins at the foot of the cross. Christ is the Conquering King, and we are the captives in His train, set free from sin and death. But that is just the first step of faith. Going all in is following in the footsteps of Jesus wherever they may lead us, including down the Via Dolorosa, the "Way of Grief." But even on the way of suffering, God is leading us in triumphal procession.

For four centuries, the Israelites suffered as slaves in the land of Egypt. Then God raised up a deliverer named Moses. With ten miraculous signs, the triumphal procession out of Egypt began. But by the time the Israelites reached the Red Sea, it seemed like a death march. And the Rea Sea was the dead end, literally. But God made a way where there was no way. He parted the waters so Israel could march through on dry ground. And what seemed like certain defeat turned into their most notable victory.

If you plot the route the Israelites traveled, it looks like the blind leading the blind. What should have taken eleven days ended up taking forty years! But despite all the detours and delays, it was still a triumphal procession. The path through the Jordan River was their Via Triumphalis. And from Jericho onward, they went from victory to victory.

THE ELEMENT OF SURPRISE

Moses lived on the back side of the desert staring at the backside of sheep for four decades. His life was defined by monotony until he had an epiphany. On a day that started out like the 14,600 days before, Moses spotted a burning bush out of the corner of his eye. Then he heard a voice from out of the bush calling his name.

The burning bush reveals the playful side of God's personality. You better expect the unexpected because God is predictably unpredictable. But this one takes the cake, doesn't it? A talking bush is about as absurd as a talking donkey. Oh, wait, God did that too!

You can't read the Gospels without realizing that this part

of the Father's personality is personified in Jesus. Jesus walked on water, turned water into wine, and healed a shriveled hand on the Sabbath. Those are certainly miracles of the first order, but there is a playful nature to them as well. I don't think it's sacrilegious to call them holy pranks with a providential purpose.

And that brings us back to the burning bush.

Why did God reveal Himself that way?

It's for the same reason that the angels announced the birth of the Messiah to night-shift shepherds instead of religious scholars. It's for the same reason that the Messiah was born to a peasant couple who came from the wrong side of the tracks instead of a priestly family in the holy city.

God loves the element of surprise!

HOLY GROUND

Jewish scholars used to debate why God revealed Himself to Moses in the middle of nowhere—a burning bush on the back side of the desert. Why not a highly populated or religiously significant place? Why would God go out of His way to go out of His way? The consensus was that God wanted to show "that no place on earth, not even a thornbush, is devoid of the Presence."

God is everywhere to be found.

God is where you want to be.

God is where it's at.

The theological word is *immanence*. And it's the complement to *transcendence*.

He is God Most High.

He is also God Most Nigh.

One of the benedictions we pronounce at the end of our services captures this name and this concept: *When you leave this place, you don't leave God's presence. You take His presence with you wherever you go.*

You are standing on holy ground.

The holy ground is not the Promised Land. It's right here, right now. Every place on which you set your foot is Promised Land.

When you go all in with God, you never know how or when or where He might show up. But you can live in holy anticipation, knowing that God can invade the reality of your life at any given moment and change everything for eternity.

WHO AM I?

When God revealed His plan to Moses, Moses objected to the Almighty. He detailed a litany of excuses ranging from his lack of credentials to his stuttering problem. He summarized his insecurities by simply saying, "Who am I?" But that's the wrong question. It's not about *who* you are. It's about *whose* you are! And I love the Almighty's answer: "I AM WHO I AM." God answers his questions by revealing His name. And He also offers this reassurance: "I will be with you."

That's all we need to know, isn't it?

If God is for us, who can be against us?

God plus one equals a supermajority.

His name is the solution to every problem.

His name is the answer to every question.

His name calms every fear, seals every prayer, and wins every battle.

At His name, angels bow and demons quake.

At His name, our sin is vindicated and our authority is validated.

It's not about who you are!

God has chosen to accomplish His purposes through ordinary people. He loves being in co-mission with His children. So He invites us into His plans and purposes. But we've got to throw down our staff to get in the game.

LET GO AND LET GOD

Then the LORD asked him, "What is that in your hand?"
"A shepherd's staff," Moses replied.
"Throw it down on the ground," the LORD told him.
So Moses threw down the staff, and it turned into a snake!

Throwing down your staff is letting go and letting God. And that's counterintuitive for those of us who are control freaks.

I naturally grip the golf club a little tighter when I want to drive the ball a little farther, but it has the opposite effect. The key to a long drive is loosening your grip.

And so it is with everything.

The staff represented Moses's identity and security as a shepherd. It was the way Moses made a living. It was also the way he protected himself and his flock. So when God told Moses to throw it down, He was asking Moses to let go of who he was and what he had.

It was Moses's all-in moment.

What are you holding on to? Or maybe I should ask, What

are you not willing to let go of? If you aren't willing to let go, then you don't control whatever it is that you are holding on to. It controls you. And if you don't throw it down, your staff will forever remain a staff. It will always be what it currently is. But if you have the courage to throw down your staff, it will become the lightning rod of God's miraculous power, not because you threw it, but because of the One who'll change it.

WHAT'S IN YOUR HAND?

What is that in your hand?

That is the question the Lord asked of Moses.

It's the same question He asks of us.

You may be tempted to say, *Just a staff.* You may be tempted to think, *I can't make much of a difference anyway.* And you can't as long as you hang on to what you have. But if you put the two fish you have in your hands into God's hands, God can feed five thousand with it.

In God's economy, 5 + 2 doesn't equal 7. It equals 5,000, R12. The disciples didn't think two fish and five loaves could make much of a difference, but they obviously underestimated the original Iron Chef. When dinner was done, there were twelve basketfuls left over. There was more left over than they originally started with.

If the little boy had held on to the two fish and five loaves, they would have remained what they were. But by putting them into the hands of Jesus, those two fish and five loaves turned into the miraculous feeding of the multitude!

What's in your hand?

You can hang on to it and see what you can do.

Or you can hand it over and see what God can do.

And when everything is said and done, what you don't share is lost forever. But what you put into the hands of God becomes an eternal keepsake.

Throw down your staff.

FOURTEEN

TAKE A STAND

*"King Nebuchadnezzar, we do not need to defend
ourselves before you in this matter. If we are thrown
into the blazing furnace, the God we serve is able to
deliver us from it, and he will deliver us from Your
Majesty's hand. But even if he does not, we want you
to know, Your Majesty, that we will not serve your
gods or worship the image of gold you have set up."*

Daniel 3:16–18

Few things are as life-changing as a near-death experience.
I've experienced it personally, having survived for several
days on a respirator after emergency surgery to repair rup-
tured intestines. And I've experienced it vicariously with my
twenty-nine-year-old brother-in-law, Matt, who had open-
heart surgery followed by emergency surgery two weeks later.

Death is a mirror that gives us a glimpse of who we
really are.

Death is a rearview mirror that puts the past into
perspective.

The closer you come to death, the clearer and farther

you can see. Nothing recalibrates priorities faster than a cancer screening, a car accident, or a phone call from a military chaplain. Important things become all-important. And the unimportant things are revealed as insignificant. You realize that every day should be lived like the first day and last day of your life! You've got to make every day count.

In my experience, near-death experiences turn into near-life experiences. I actually celebrate two birthdays every year. One is my biological birthday, November 5. The other is the day I should have died, July 23. The second is more meaningful than the first.

I'm living on borrowed time. The truth is, all of us are!

Near-death experiences often become the defining moments in our lives. And I don't know of a near-death experience that is more dramatic than that of Shadrach, Meshach, and Abednego.

DEATH SENTENCE

It was a death sentence.

Shadrach, Meshach, and Abednego knew that if they refused to bow down to the ninety-foot-tall statue of King Nebuchadnezzar, they would be executed. But these three Jewish expats obviously feared God more than they feared death itself. They would rather die by the flame than dishonor God.

It was all or nothing.

It was now or never.

It was life or death.

To be honest, I could have come up with a dozen

rationalizations to justify bowing down. *I'm bowing on the outside, but I'm not bowing on the inside. I'll ask for forgiveness right after I get back up. My fingers are crossed. I'm only breaking one of the Ten Commandments. What good am I to God if I'm dead?*

When we compromise our integrity, we don't leave room for divine intervention. When we stay safe, we take God out of the equation. When we try to manipulate a situation, we miss out on the miracle.

If Shadrach, Meshach, and Abednego had compromised their integrity and bowed down to the statue, they would have been delivered from the fiery furnace. But it would have been by Nebuchadnezzar, not by God. And it would have been *from*, not *through*. They would have forfeited their testimony by failing the test. And while they would have saved their lives, they would have sacrificed their integrity.

It was their integrity that triggered the miracle.

It was their integrity that allowed God to show up and show off.

It was their integrity that was their fire insurance and life insurance.

EPIC INTEGRITY

To bow or not to bow?

That is the question.

And while I can't imagine anyone's employer constructing a ninety-foot-tall statue to himself or herself, I wouldn't be surprised if they ask you to cut a corner here or cook a number there. Don't bow down. Lose your job before you lose your integrity!

It was integrity that got Shadrach, Meshach, and Abednego in trouble with Nebuchadnezzar, but it was that same integrity that found them favor with God. So which is it? To bow or not to bow? Because you can't have it both ways! I'd rather get in trouble with King Nebuchadnezzar than get in trouble with God.

When we violate our conscience by compromising our integrity, we put our reputation at risk. We also become our own advocate because we step outside the boundaries of God's good, pleasing, and perfect will. But when we obey God, we come under the umbrella of His protective authority. He is our Advocate. And it's His reputation that is at stake. If we don't give the Enemy a foothold, God won't let him touch a hair on our head.

Not a hair on their heads was singed, and their clothing was not scorched. They didn't even smell of smoke!

Integrity won't keep us from getting thrown into the fiery furnace, but it can keep us from getting burned. And it won't just protect us. It will also convict the people around us. When we live according to our convictions, God will show up and show off in crazy ways. The Redeemer wants to rescue us, but by faith we have to put ourselves in that precarious position.

DON'T PLAY DEFENSE

Who are you going to offend?

That is one of the most important decisions you'll ever make!

If you fear man, you'll offend God.

If you fear God, you'll offend man.

Jesus certainly wasn't afraid of offending Pharisees. In fact, He turned it into an art form. And I've turned it into one of my maxims: *thou shalt offend Pharisees!* Or in this instance, thou shalt offend Nebuchadnezzar!

Shadrach, Meshach, and Abednego did not want to offend the king. After all, their positions of power were promotions granted by Nebuchadnezzar himself. They owed him their livelihood. So not bowing down to his statue was like slapping the hand that feeds you, but the only other option was slapping the hand of God.

So who are we going to offend?

I've discovered that the more influence someone has, the larger the target on their back becomes. People will take potshots at you. Trust me, I've had my fair share as an author and a pastor. Here's how I try to handle it.

I don't play defense. Life is too short to spend all of my time and energy defending myself. God is my Judge and my Jury. I live by a variation of the maxim Abraham Lincoln lived by: "You can please all of the people some of the time, and some of the people all of the time, but you can't please all of the people all of the time." Of course, it's particularly difficult when the person's name is Nebuchadnezzar! But no matter how you slice it, the fear of God is the beginning of wisdom, and the fear of man is the beginning of foolishness.

The book of Proverbs contains these words:

It is to one's glory to overlook an offense.

I've had to stand on that promise more than once! In fact, it's one of the most-circled promises in my Bible. My goal is to be nearly impossible to offend because of the grace of God. If God has forgiven me for every offense, how can I take offense at someone else's sin? I know that if I take offense, then I get defensive, and I stop playing offense with my life. And that is exactly how the Enemy neutralizes us.

Jesus didn't defend Himself before Pilate. He didn't defend Himself when the soldiers whipped His back, spit in His face, and put a crown of thorns on His head. He didn't defend Himself when nails were driven through His hands and feet.

Jesus had a legion of angels at His beck and call, but He didn't dial 911. He didn't defend Himself, and He didn't take offense either. Instead, the Advocate interceded for His executioners: "Father, forgive them, for they do not know what they are doing."

NINETY-FOOT-TALL EGO

Shadrach, Meshach, and Abednego did not defend themselves. They simply acted according to their convictions. That's what no fear is all about. It's refusing to bow down to what's wrong. And even more, it's standing up for what's right. And when Nebuchadnezzar witnessed their uncompromising integrity, the king himself made a proclamation of faith. Unfortunately, he may have taken it a little too far, because he then threatened to tear from limb to limb anyone who didn't bow down to the God of Shadrach, Meshach, and Abednego.

I think it's safe to say that anyone who builds a ninety-foot-tall statue of themselves is probably compensating for something. This statue is the epitome of pride. And

Nebuchadnezzar certainly ranks high on the list of history's egomaniacs. But we all have a little Nebuchadnezzar in us.

We seek worship in more subtle ways. We exaggerate on our résumé. We put down others behind their back. And we tell white lies to hide the gray areas in our lives.

If you don't find your identity and security in what Christ has accomplished for you on the cross, you will try to hide your insecurities behind your hypocrisies.

You will try to fight your own battles.

You will try to create your own opportunities.

You will try to establish your own reputation.

And you'll quickly discover that manipulating is exhausting.

Just ask Saul. Scripture says he kept a jealous eye on David. Saul was cross-eyed—he was more concerned about his reputation than God's reputation.

Two verses point to two defining moments in his downfall.

Then Saul built an altar to the LORD; it was the first of the altars he built to the LORD.

And then one chapter later:

Saul went to the town of Carmel to set up a monument to himself.

Somewhere between 1 Samuel 14:35 and 1 Samuel 15:12, Saul stopped building altars to God and started building monuments to himself. And the prophet Samuel saw right through the smoke screen: "Although you may think little of yourself, are you not the leader of the tribes of Israel?"

You know who builds monuments to themselves? Those who think little of themselves!

There is a fine line between *Thy kingdom come* and *my kingdom come*. If you cross the line, your relationship with God is self-serving.

You aren't serving God. You are using God.

You aren't building altars to God. You are building monuments to yourself.

And there is a name for that: idolatry.

TAKE A STAND

There comes a moment when you need to take a stand for what's right, take a stand for God. This was that moment for Shadrach, Meshach, and Abednego. And these are the moments that define our integrity.

Is there anything you are bowing to?

Then it's time to take a stand.

And it always starts with the little things.

More than all of his cumulative victories on the golf course, Bobby Jones is famous for a one-shot penalty at the 1925 United States Open. He inadvertently touched his golf ball and assessed himself a one-stroke penalty, even though no one else saw him touch the ball. But Bobby Jones couldn't violate his conscience. He assessed himself a penalty and ultimately lost the Open by that one stroke.

When tournament officials tried to compliment him for his integrity, Jones simply said, "You might as well praise me for not breaking into banks. There is only one way to play this game." That's epic integrity.

And that's something to be celebrated. Integrity is the only thing that doesn't depreciate over time. Nothing takes longer to build than a godly reputation. And nothing is destroyed more quickly by one stroke of sin. That's why it must be celebrated and protected above all else.

Your integrity is your legacy.

Your integrity is your destiny.

Take a stand.

FIFTEEN

THIRTY PIECES
OF SILVER

*Then Judas Iscariot, one of the twelve disciples, went
to the leading priests and asked, "How much will you
pay me to betray Jesus to you?"
And they gave him thirty pieces of silver.*
MATTHEW 26:14–15 NLT

Judas couldn't keep his hand out of the cookie jar. He
didn't just sell out by betraying Jesus for thirty pieces of
silver—Judas never bought in. And it's evidenced by his lack
of integrity from the get-go.

*He was a thief, and having charge of the moneybag he
used to help himself to what was put into it.*

The betrayal of Jesus by Judas wasn't a spur-of-the-moment
mistake. He betrayed Jesus each and every time he pilfered the
money pot. And while most of us can't imagine pickpocketing

Jesus, we shortchange Him in a thousand different ways. We rob God of the glory He demands and deserves by not living up to our full, God-given potential.

Sin always overpromises and underdelivers, while righteousness pays dividends for eternity. Yet we sell out.

Esau sold his birthright for a bowl of stew.

Samson sold his secret for a one-night stand.

Judas sold his soul for thirty pieces of silver.

What were they thinking? The answer is, they weren't. Nothing is more illogical than sin. It's the epitome of poor judgment. It's temporary insanity with eternal consequences. And we have no alibi, save the cross of Jesus Christ.

It's not worth it, and we know it.

Yet we do it.

We sell out for so little instead of going all in for so much.

C. S. Lewis described our tendency to sell God short:

It would seem that Our Lord finds our desires, not too strong, but too weak. We are half-hearted creatures, fooling about with drink and sex and ambition when infinite joy is offered us, like an ignorant child who wants to go on making mud pies in a slum because he cannot imagine what is meant by the offer of a holiday at the sea. We are far too easily pleased.

Thirty pieces of silver. That was Judas's price point. Jewish readers would have recognized it as the exact amount to be paid if a slave was accidentally killed under Mosaic law. Judas sold his soul for the replacement value of a slave.

The silver coins were most likely sanctuary shekels, since he was paid off by the chief priests. And while some estimates range higher, each coin may have been worth as little as seventy-two cents! So in today's currency, Judas betrayed Jesus for $21.60.

A LITTLE JUDAS

We know very little about Judas from Scripture, but theories abound. Some scholars suggest Judas was a weak-willed coward with a manipulative wife pulling the strings. Others believe Judas betrayed Jesus out of pure greed. And some suggest he had revolutionary aspirations. He wanted a political savior, and when Jesus didn't meet his expectations, he went AWOL.

And we do the same thing, don't we? When God doesn't conform to our expectations, we're tempted to betray what we believe in. Like Judas, we're in it for what we can get out of it. So when God doesn't grant our wishes like a divine genie in a bottle, we are tempted to turn our back on Him.

How do you react when God doesn't meet your expectations? If you have truly accepted the invitation to follow Jesus, you'll keep going on through hurricanes, hail, and hazardous conditions. If you have simply invited Him to follow you, you'll bail out at the first sign of bad weather.

There is a little Judas in all of us. And any of us are capable of betraying God if we allow the fear of people to erode the fear of God, selfish ambition to strong-arm godly ambition, or sinful desires to short-circuit God-ordained passions.

LONG SHADOWS

The betrayal of Judas was foretold by the prophet Zechariah five hundred years before it happened, but that prophecy doesn't mean we should fall victim to fatalism. God has given us free will. So for better or for worse, the choice is ours.

History turns on a dime.

The dime is our defining decisions.

Those decisions, right or wrong, determine our destiny.

Some defining decisions are obvious, like choosing a career or choosing a spouse. But most are made in the shadows, like Judas's. Of course, they eventually come into the light. And it's those defining decisions that cast the longest shadows.

I think of Joseph resisting the flirtatious overtures of Potiphar's wife. He had no idea how that one choice would alter his life and the course of history. And doing the right thing didn't pay any dividends for seventeen years. In fact, it seemed to backfire when Joseph landed in jail. But our decisions, right or wrong, always catch up with us sooner or later.

I think of David making a split-second decision not to kill King Saul when he had him cornered near the Crags of the Wild Goats. He could have claimed self-defense. And no one would have seen him do it. No one, that is, except for the All-Seeing Eye!

Of course, David made his fair share of bad decisions too. He did a little window peeping from the palace porch. And after sleeping with Bathsheba, he tried to cover it up by having Uriah, her husband, killed.

Bad decisions usually lead to worse decisions. After Judas betrayed Jesus, he made the worst decision and last decision of his life. He ended his life by hanging himself from a tree in a potter's field. It's more than a sad ending. It's a standing warning.

The good news is that God can forgive our bad decisions. And one good decision can totally change the trajectory of our lives. And that one good decision will lead to better decisions. But it starts by making the right decision when no one is looking.

What defining decision do you need to make?

What risk do you need to take?

What sacrifice do you need to make?

AND SO LIFE IS

In 1931, the Irish author George William Russell penned a cryptic piece of poetry titled "Germinal."

> In ancient shadows and twilights
> Where childhood had strayed
> The world's great sorrows were born
> And its heroes were made.
> In the lost boyhood of Judas
> Christ was betrayed.

Judas didn't decide to betray Christ after following Him for three years. The seeds of betrayal were planted in the soil of his youth. That certainly doesn't excuse what Judas did. And he could have decided not to do it. But our most important choices, good and bad, often have the longest genealogies.

The Austrian psychotherapist Alfred Adler was famous for beginning counseling sessions with new clients by asking, "What is your earliest memory?" No matter how the patient answered, Adler responded, "And so life is."

We know next to nothing about Judas as a toddler, teenager, or twentysomething. But I'm guessing he threw temper tantrums when he didn't get what he wanted, because that infantile self-centeredness was still evident when the woman with the alabaster jar anointed Jesus. Judas had the gall to make a stink.

> *"That perfume was worth a year's wages. It should have been sold and the money given to the poor."*

Judas should have been up for an Oscar with that performance. He could not have cared less for the poor. That perfume would have fetched a pretty penny. A lot more than $21.60!

It is much easier to *act* like a Christian than it is to *react* like one!

Are we any different?

The Talmud teaches that there are four kinds of people in the world.

The first person says, *What's yours is mine.*

The second person says, *What's yours is yours.*

The third person says, *What's mine is mine.*

And the fourth person says, *What's mine is yours.*

Which one are you?

THE SECOND SIN

The original sin, committed by Adam and Eve, was buying into the Enemy's lie that God was holding out on them. They ate from the tree of the knowledge of good and evil because they did not believe that God was all in. And the apple didn't fall far from the proverbial tree. So the second sin recorded in Scripture, and the first sin outside the garden of Eden, is a stepchild of the original sin.

Abel had no fear.

He brought God the best of the best—his choice lambs.

But Cain held out.

He gave God leftovers—the worst part of his harvest.

Nothing has changed.

The choice is still ours to make.

There is no middle ground.

Isn't that the lesson to be learned from Ananias and Sapphira? They gifted the proceeds from a property sale to the church, but God struck them dead. Why? Because they bald-faced lied about being all in. They claimed they had anted up everything, but they kept a little pocket change.

The true value of an offering isn't measured by how much we give. It's measured by how much we keep. That's why the widow who only gave two small copper coins was honored for her generosity. She gave less than anybody else, but she kept nothing for herself. That's why Jesus honored the little boy who gave five loaves and two fish. It wasn't much, but it was everything he had.

By definition, a sacrifice must involve sacrifice. Cain gave what he did not want or could not use. He kept the best and gave the worst. And that's never been good enough for the All in All.

GOLD, FRANKINCENSE, AND MYRRH

The story of the Magi is often relegated to a Christmas homily, but the Wise Men stand in stark contrast to Judas. Judas sold out for some silver coins. The Magi bought in with gifts of gold.

At first glance, it seems like the Magi bring the wrong gifts to this baby shower, doesn't it?

It reminds me of a little quip I came across titled "The Three Wise Women."

Do you know what would have happened if it had been three wise women instead of three wise men? They would have asked for directions, arrived on time, helped deliver the baby, cleaned the stable, made a casserole, and brought practical gifts.

Gold, frankincense, and myrrh seem like misguided gifts, but stop and think about it. How does a minimum-wage carpenter who just paid a huge tax bill fund a trip to a foreign country? These gifts were just what Mary and Joseph needed. They were their golden ticket to Egypt. And it's the only way they could have escaped the genocide that ensued. Those gifts saved their lives!

Now let me connect the dots.

The Magi's gifts were Mary and Joseph's miracle!

And the same is true for us. Giving is one way we get in on God's miracles. Your gifts of gold, frankincense, and myrrh could translate into someone else's miracle.

Maybe it's time to quit looking for the easy way out and go the extra mile.

Maybe it's time to quit holding out and start doubling down.

Maybe it's time to quit expecting Jesus to follow you and make the decision to follow him.

PART FIVE

NOT AFRAID

SIXTEEN

THE IDOL THAT
PROVOKES TO
JEALOUSY

*The Spirit lifted me up between earth and heaven
and in visions of God he took me to Jerusalem, to the
entrance of the north gate of the inner court, where
the idol that provokes to jealousy stood.*
EZEKIEL 8:3

God is not jealous *of* anything. He can't be. The Almighty is all-sufficient. But the Creator is jealous *for* everything because it all belongs to Him.

Every blade of grass.

Every drop of water.

Every grain of sand.

The character of God is revealed by the names of God. One of those names is revealed to Moses on Mount Sinai:

"Do not worship any other god, for the LORD, whose name is Jealous, is a jealous God."

Did you catch the double emphasis?

God isn't just jealous. He is doubly jealous. And when God says something more than once, you need to think twice about what it means.

You don't belong to God once. You belong to God twice.

Once by virtue of creation.

Twice by virtue of redemption.

He gave us life via creation. And when we were dead in our sin, He gave us eternal life via redemption. We don't owe Him one life. We owe Him two lives! And that is why God is doubly jealous.

Jealousy isn't a character trait that we sing about or write about often. But God's jealousy is a beautiful expression of God's love. It's a jealous love that wants all of you—all to Himself. And if you've ever been in love, you know it's the most passionate form of love there is.

THE END OF ME

I don't think I understood this dimension of love until I became a husband and a father. I'm jealous for my wife. She belongs to me, and I belong to her. Marriage is not a fifty-fifty proposition. I vowed all of me to all of her. It was *for better for worse, for richer for poorer, in sickness and in health.*

As a pastor, I often help couples craft their wedding vows. One of my favorite lines is this one: *holding nothing back.* It's no fear. Marriage is not a compromise. It's putting ourselves on the altar at the altar. There is no more *me*. There is only *we*. Anything less is adulterous.

I am jealous for my wife. If you mess with her, you mess with me. And I'll take you down! My love for my wife is protective and possessive—in the big things and the small things.

Jealousy, in the context of holy matrimony, is the most beautiful expression of love on earth. And when you see yourself for who you really are, the bride of Christ, you begin to understand the tenacity and veracity of jealous love. You also begin to see idolatry for what it really is: adultery.

SEVEN BILLION < THREE

I want my kids to love God first and foremost, but my secondary prayer is that they'd love their mom and dad too! No thought is more painful to me as a parent than the thought of my kids not loving me the way I love them, but that is their prerogative. And it probably won't be until they have children of their own that they will fully appreciate the way their mom and I love them.

If you said to me that two out of my three kids would love me, I would not be satisfied with 66.7 percent. I would be devastated. I don't love my kids equally. I love them uniquely. And that's how God loves us. His love for you is not just unconditional. His love for you is absolutely unique.

For God so loved the world that He gave His only begotten Son.

Most of us have memorized John 3:16, but we've never personalized it. We know He loves everyone, but because there are billions of people on the planet, we feel a little lost in the mix. You can probably understand how devastated I'd feel if one of my kids didn't love me, but have you ever stopped to consider the simple fact that seven billion to an infinite God is a lot less than three is to me!

Just as your love for God is unique, so is His love for you. God's love is not divided seven billion ways. He loves all of you with all of Himself. The only question that remains is this:

Is He your pearl of great price?

SEX GOD

In the book by the same name, the prophet Ezekiel has a vision of an idol that is dubbed "the idol that provokes to jealousy." Scholars believe the idol referenced is the Canaanite goddess of fertility.

It was their sex god.

I know it seems a little foreign and a little naive to read about ancient pagans carving their own idols and then bowing down to whittled wood. But are we any different? Any better?

Have you been to Las Vegas lately? The god of lust is worshiped openly and freely. But the fact that pornography is a one-hundred-billion dollar industry is proof that the god of lust is also worshiped secretly and addictively everywhere else. What I'm getting at is this: we're still bowing down to the Canaanite goddess of fertility. And like every other idol, it must be dethroned. We have to stage a coup d'état against the idolatry.

What is your idol that provokes to jealousy?

Idolatry is anything that keeps you afraid.

Idolatry is anything that keeps God from being your All in All.

Identifying your idols starts with looking at the way you spend your time and spend your money. My calendar and my checkbook don't lie. They reveal what my true priorities are. They will also reveal the idol that provokes to jealousy.

HIDDEN ROOMS

Idolatry isn't a problem. It's *the* problem.

Sin is just a symptom. Idolatry is the root cause.

You can't just confess the sin. You also have to dethrone the idol.

The Canaanite goddess of sex was the most visible idol in the temple, but it was just the tip of the idolatry iceberg. When Ezekiel peered through a peephole into a hidden room within the temple, he saw crawling things and unclean animals portrayed on the walls like ancient hieroglyphics.

What's etched on the walls of your mind?

What's concealed in the hidden room of your heart?

All of us have hidden rooms—the secret sin that no one sees except the All-Seeing Eye. It's what you do when no one is looking. It's who you are when no one else is present. It's the place where we conceal our most precious idols. And the Enemy wants you to keep your secret sin a secret. That's how he blackmails us.

Our church recently filmed a series of short documentaries. Week after week, courageous individuals shared some of their deepest hurts and greatest struggles. With each testimony, our church grew in grace. When a member of our staff shared about his secret addiction to gay pornography, people opened the door to their hidden rooms. Shame rushed out and grace rushed in. In the book of Revelation, we read that Jesus stands at the door and knocks. A relationship begins when we open the front door, but it doesn't end there. He knocks on the closet doors too!

Just as the Jewish temple had an outer court and inner court, our hearts have an outer court and inner court. It's not enough to invite Jesus into the outer court. You have to let Him into the inner court. He wants to renovate every corner and crevice of your heart, but you have to open the door to your hidden room. And in some instances, He does a complete gut job.

C. S. Lewis described it in similar terms:

> Imagine yourself as a living house. God comes in to rebuild that house. At first, perhaps, you can understand what he is doing. He is getting the drains right and stopping the leaks in the roof and so on . . . But presently he starts knocking the house about in a way that hurts abominably and does not seem to make sense. What on earth is He up to? The explanation is that He is building quite a different house from the one you thought of—throwing out a new wing here, putting on an extra floor there, running up towers, making courtyards. You thought you were going to be made into a decent little cottage: but He is building a palace. He intends to come and live in it himself.

THE GORDIAN KNOT

After revealing what was in the hidden rooms, Ezekiel encounters one more idol at the entrance to the north gate of the temple. He saw women mourning Tammuz, the Babylonian fertility god of spring. The key word is *mourning*. If you want to identify your idols, you need to reverse engineer your emotions. Trace the trail of your tears, cheers, or fears. Follow it all the way to the trailhead, and you'll come face-to-face with the idols in your life.

What makes you mad or sad or glad?

What ruins or makes your day?

What triggers your strongest emotional reactions?

That's your Tammuz.

The indictment against the Israelites isn't just that they were having an emotional affair with a false god. They were flatline in their feelings toward the very God who created them. If your deepest feelings are reserved for something other than Almighty God, then that something other is an emotional idol. I'm not saying you shouldn't get excited about your favorite team, favorite hobby, or favorite food. But if you get more excited about material things than the simple yet profound fact that your sin was nailed to the cross by the sinless Son of God, then you're bowing down to Tammuz.

How you show emotion isn't the issue.

Neither is *when* or *where*.

The real issue is *why*.

Does your heart break for the things that break the heart of God?

The estimated number of unique human emotions range as high as four hundred, but no matter how many there are, we're called to love God with every single one of them. That's what it means to love God with all our heart.

The distance between your head and your heart is only twelve inches, but it's the difference between information and transformation. It's not enough to invite Jesus into your mind. You have to open the door to your heart of hearts. No door can remain locked. Even the door to your hidden room.

Nothing entangles the emotions like sin. And if you sin long enough, it feels like a Gordian knot that seems impossible to untangle. But Jesus Christ went to the cross to undo what you have done. He broke the curse of sin so you can break the cycle of sin.

I don't know what you've built around your heart, but God wants to do a gut job. It starts by letting him in.

Isn't it time?

Time to answer the knock on the door of your heart.

Time to open the door and invite Jesus in.

It may not be safe, but it is time.

SEVENTEEN

ONE DECISION AWAY

Few Americans have stamped the collective consciousness of our country like Jonathan Edwards. He was an intellectual prodigy, entering Yale University at the age of twelve. And he is buried at Princeton University, where he served as president until his death in 1758. Edwards was the author of dozens of volumes, both theological and inspirational. His biography of David Brainerd has inspired countless missionaries to go all in with God. And it was Jonathan Edwards who sparked America's First Great Awakening with his sermon, "Sinners in the Hands of an Angry God." But his greatest legacy may be his progeny, which include more than 300 ministers and missionaries, 120 university professors, 60 authors, 30 judges, 14 college presidents, 3 members of Congress, and 1 vice president.

That legacy, like every spiritual genealogy, traces back to a defining moment.

On January 12, 1723, Jonathan Edwards made a written consecration of himself to God. He wrote it out longhand in his diary and revisited it often over the years.

> I made a solemn dedication of myself to God, and wrote it down; giving up myself, and all that I had to

God; to be for the future, in no respect, my own; to act as one that had no right to himself, in any respect. And solemnly vowed, to take God for my whole portion and felicity; looking on nothing else, as any part of my happiness, nor acting as if it were.

If you don't hold out on God, God will not hold out on you.

There is nothing God cannot do in and through a person who is fully consecrated to Him. We want to do amazing things for God, but that isn't our job. That's God's job. Our job is to fully surrender all that we have and all that we are to the Lord Jesus Christ. And if we do our job, God will most certainly do His.

So we stand on the same three-thousand-year-old promise the Israelites did:

> *"Consecrate yourselves, for tomorrow the LORD will do amazing things among you."*

God wants to do amazing things.

He's simply waiting for us to consecrate ourselves.

You are one unsafe decision away from a totally different life.

What will you do?

NOTES

CHAPTER 1

3 *"A.W. Milne was one"*: From a lecture by Dr. Howard Foltz, missiology professor at Regent Universty, 2002.

CHAPTER 2

7 *"The world has yet to see"*: Quoted in William R. Moody, *The Life of Dwight L. Moody* (New York: Revell, 1900), 134; see Mark Fackler, "The World Has Yet to See . . . ," *Christianity Today* (January 1, 1990), www.ctlibrary.com/ch/1990/issue25/2510.html (accessed February 11, 2013).

8 *"Consecrate yourselves"*: Joshua 3:5.

CHAPTER 3

11 *"In AD 44, King Herod ordered"*: James's martyrdom is the only one mentioned in Scripture. See Acts 12:1–2.

11 *"And so the bloodbath began"*: See Grant R. Jeffrey, *The Signature of God* (Frontier Research, 1996), 254–57.

13 *"God made him who had no sin"*: 2 Corinthians 5:21.

14 *"No good thing does God"*: Psalm 84:11 ESV.

15 *"the Rich Young Ruler"*: Luke 18:18–30.

15 *"What am I still missing?"*: Matthew 19:20 CEB.

16 *"parable of the bags of gold"*: Matthew 25:14–30.

17 *"If you want to be perfect"*: Matthew 19:21.

CHAPTER 4

24 *"awarded the Medal of Honor"*: Quoted in Thomas A. Desjardin, *Stand Firm Ye Boys of Maine: The 20th Maine and the Gettysburg Campaign*, 15th anniv. ed. (New York: Oxford University Press, 2009), 148.

24 *"I had deep within me"*: Quoted in Andy Andrews, *The Butterfly Effect: How Your Life Matters* (Nashville: Nelson, 2010), 20–21.

26 *"Their leader had no real knowledge"*: Ibid., 20.

CHAPTER 5

29 *"God tested Abraham"*: Genesis 22:1.

31 *"It was God who gave"*: Some scholars infer from Ezekiel 28:13–17 that Lucifer led the angelic choirs in heaven. While that conclusion cannot be substantiated, it is one possible interpretation.

32 *"Fourteen years' worth of work"*: Phil Vischer, *Me, Myself, & Bob: A True Story About God, Dreams, and Talking Vegetables* (Nashville: Nelson, 2006), 196.

32 *"If God gives you a dream"*: Ibid., 234.

34 *"I am no longer my own"*: *The Book of Offices* (London: Methodist Publishing House, 1936), 57.

CHAPTER 6

41 *"tax collector who put his faith in Christ"*: Luke 19:1–10.

41 *"prostitute who anointed Jesus"*: Mark 14:1–9.

41 *"revival that broke out in Ephesus"*: Acts 19:17–20.

41 *"made a $3,739,972.50 statement"*: Based on minimum wage in Washington, DC.

42 *"Seek me and live"*: Amos 5:4–6.

42 *"ever-present help"*: Psalm 46:1.

43 *"From the days of John the Baptist"*: Matthew 11:12 NIV (1984 ed.).

45 *"That's twice as many"*: See David Pyles, "A Double Portion of Thy Spirit," www.bcbsr.com/survey/eli.html (accessed February 14, 2013).

47 *"Elisha gets extra credit for making"*: 2 Kings 2:14; 4:34; 6:6.

CHAPTER 7

56 *"Wherever this gospel is preached"*: Matthew 26:13.

57 *"If this man were a prophet"*: Luke 7:39.

59 *"True spirituality is"*: Michael Yaconelli, *Messy Spirituality*, rev. ed. (Grand Rapids: Zondervan, 2007), 46.

CHAPTER 8

65 *"Eternity will not be long enough"*: A. W. Tozer, *The Pursuit of God* (Radford, Va.: Wilder, 2008), 30.

66 *"We need to study the Word"*: 2 Timothy 2:15.
66 *"Well done, good and faithful"*: Matthew 25:23.

CHAPTER 9
70 *"Come, let's go over"*: 1 Samuel 14:1.
71 *"But if they say"*: 1 Samuel 14:10
72 *"Perhaps the Lord will act"*: 1 Samuel 14:6.
72 *"So on that day"*: 1 Samuel 14:23.
75 *"I will build my church"*: Matthew 16:18.
77 *"A pair of psychologists"*: William J. Gehring and Adrian R. Willoughby, "The Medial Frontal Cortex and the Rapid Processing of Monetary Gains and Losses," *Science* 295.5563 (March 22, 2002): 2279–2282
79 *"My conscience is taken captive"*: Henry Bettensen and Chris Maunder, eds., *Documents of the Christian Church*, 4th ed. (New York: Oxford University Press, 2011), 214.

CHAPTER 10
81 *"The internal volume of the ark"*: Christian Information Ministries, "Facts on Noah's Ark," www.ldolphin.org/cisflood.html (accessed February 14, 2013).
83 *"Noah did everything"*: Genesis 6:22.
84 *"Noah found favor"*: Genesis 6:8.
85 *"No good thing does God"*: Psalm 84:11 ESV.
89 *"I have fought the good fight"*: 2 Timothy 4:7 NLT.

CHAPTER 11
90 *"After Ehud came Shamgar"*: Judges 3:31.
91 *"And if God is for you"*: Romans 8:31.
92 *"Then I heard the voice"*: Isaiah 6:8.
95 *"On the Plains of Hesitation"*: Bob Kelly, *Worth Repeating: More Than 5,000 Classic and Contemporary Quotes* (Grand Rapids: Kregel, 2003). 169.

CHAPTER 12
103 *"Not my will"*: Luke 22:42.
103 *"Whatever you do"*: Colossians 3:23.
104 *"So whether you eat or drink"*: 1 Corinthians 10:31.
105 *"Naked I came"*: Job 1:21.

CHAPTER 13

107 *"David and Svea Flood"*: See Aggie Hurst, *Aggie: The Inspiring Story of a Girl without a Country* (Springfield, Mo.: Gospel Publishing House, 1986).

112 *"But thanks be to God"*: 2 Corinthians 2:14.

112 *"After winning a great victory"*: A great victory was considered to be a minimum of five thousand enemy troops.

113 *"And from Jericho onward"*: This thought is taken from Andrew Murray, *The Master's Indwelling* (New York: Revell, 1896), 51.

114 *"The consensus was that God"*: See Hayim Nahman Bialik and Yehoshua Hana Ravnitzky, eds., *The Book of Legends: Sefer Ha-Aggadah* (New York: Schocken, 1992), 63.

115 *"He summarized his insecurities"*: Exodus 3:11.

115 *"I AM WHO I AM"*: Exodus 3:14.

115 *"I will be with you"*: Exodus 3:12.

116 *"Then the LORD asked him"*: Exodus 4:2–3.

117 *"But if you put the two fish"*: Matthew 14:13–21.

CHAPTER 14

122 *"Not a hair on their heads"*: Daniel 3:27 NLT.

123 *"You can please all"*: For original rendition, see Alexander McClure, *"Abe" Lincoln's Yarns and Stories* (Philadelphia: International Publishing, 1901), 184: "It is true you may fool all of the people some of the time; you can even fool some of the people all of the time; but you can't fool all of the people all of the time."

123 *"It is to one's glory"*: Proverbs 19:11.

124 *"Father, forgive them"*: Luke 23:34.

125 *"Then Saul built an altar"*: 1 Samuel 14:35 NLT.

125 *"Saul went to the town"*: 1 Samuel 15:12 NLT.

125 *"Although you may think little"*: 1 Samuel 15:17 NLT.

CHAPTER 15

128 *"He was a thief"*: John 12:6 ESV.

129 *"It would seem that Our Lord"*: C. S. Lewis, *The Weight of Glory and Other Addresses* (Grand Rapids: Eerdmans, 1965), 2.

129 *"Jewish readers would have recognized"*: Exodus 21:32.

130 *"So in today's currency"*: M. R. Vincent, *Word Studies in the New Testament* (New York: Scribner's, 1887), comment on Matthew 26:16 (calculated in today's dollars).

131 *"I think of Joseph resisting"*: Genesis 39:6–8.

131 *"I think of David making"*: 1 Samuel 24:8–13.

132 *"In ancient shadows and twilights"*: George William Russell, *Vale and Other Poems* (New York: Macmillan, 1931), 28.

133 *"That perfume was worth"*: John 12:5 NLT.

135 *"Do you know what would have happened"*: Anne Jasiekiewicz, *A Laugh a Day: Jokes to Keep the Doctor Away* (Bloomington, Ind.: AuthorHouse, 2010), 18.

CHAPTER 16

140 *"Do not worship any other god"*: Exodus 34:14.

141 *"For God so loved the world"*: John 3:16 NKJV.

142 *"the idol that provokes"*: Ezekiel 8:3.

143 *"When Ezekiel peered through a peephole"*: Ezekiel 8:10.

144 *"Imagine yourself as a living house"*: C. S. Lewis, *Mere Christianity*, anniv. ed. (New York: Macmillan, 1981), 173.

145 *"He saw women mourning"*: Ezekiel 8:14.

CHAPTER 17

147 *"I made a solemn dedication"*: Edward Hickman, ed., *The Works of Jonathan Edwards* (London: William Ball, 1839), 1:56.

148 *"Consecrate yourselves"*: Joshua 3:5.